Muscular system

The muscular system includes more than 650 skeletal muscles and accounts for up to half your body weight. It is responsible for generating every movement you make. Muscles are made up of fibers that contract, or shorten, to make your heart pump blood, your lungs breathe in and out, and different parts of your body move.

W9-AVJ-757

Front

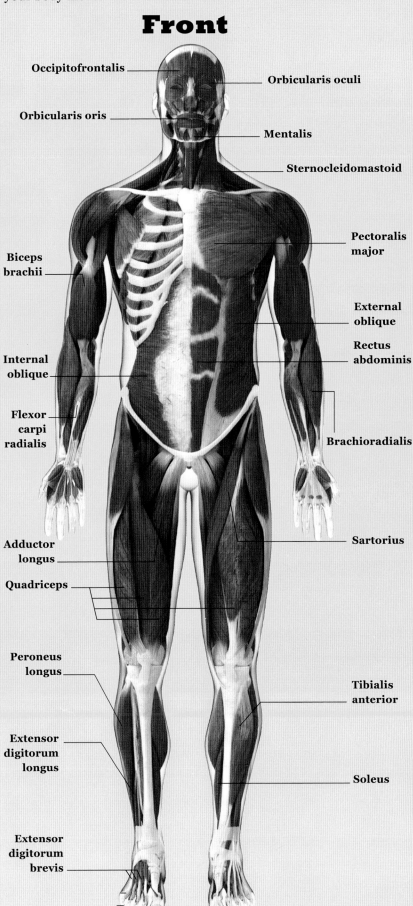

- Occipitofrontalis
- Orbicularis oculi
- Orbicularis oris
- Mentalis
- Sternocleidomastoid
- Pectoralis major
- Biceps brachii
- External oblique
- Rectus abdominis
- Internal oblique
- Flexor carpi radialis
- Brachioradialis
- Adductor longus
- Sartorius
- Quadriceps
- Peroneus longus
- Tibialis anterior
- Extensor digitorum longus
- Soleus
- Extensor digitorum brevis

Back

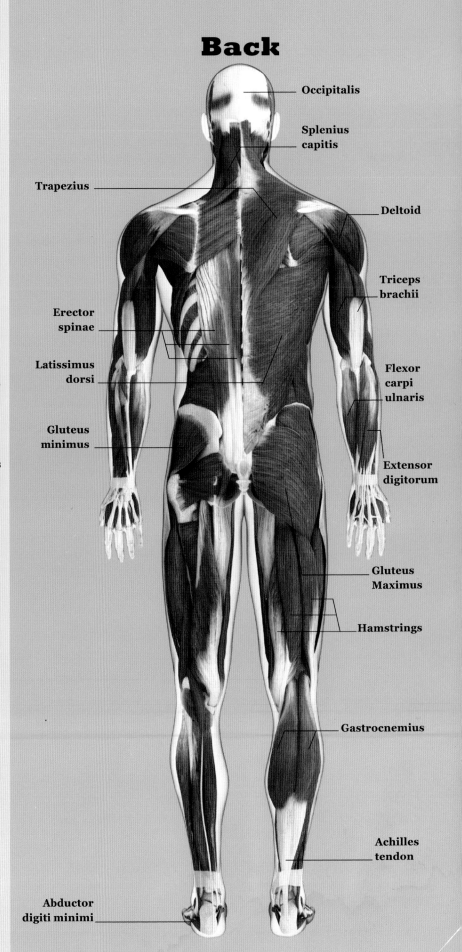

- Occipitalis
- Splenius capitis
- Trapezius
- Deltoid
- Triceps brachii
- Erector spinae
- Latissimus dorsi
- Flexor carpi ulnaris
- Gluteus minimus
- Extensor digitorum
- Gluteus Maximus
- Hamstrings
- Gastrocnemius
- Achilles tendon
- Abductor digiti minimi

DK

LONDON, NEW YORK,
MELBOURNE, MUNICH, and DELHI

Project editor Alexander Cox
Senior designers Claire Patané and Laura Roberts-Jensen
Editors Wendy Horobin, Joe Harris, Penny Smith, Leon Gray, Ben Morgan, and Lorrie Mack
Designers Sadie Thomas and Hedi Hunter
Editorial assistant Anneka Wahlhaus
Design assistant Lauren Rosier
Production editor Sean Daly
Production controller Claire Pearson
Jacket designers Jess Bentall and Nathalie Godwin
Jacket editor Mariza O'Keeffe
US editor Margaret Parrish
Art director Rachael Foster
Publishing manager Bridget Giles
Creative director Jane Bull
Publisher Mary Ling

Consultant Dr. Emma Ross

First published in the United States in 2009 by DK Publishing
375 Hudson Street, New York, New York 10014

Copyright © 2009 Dorling Kindersley Limited

09 10 11 12 13 10 9 8 7 6 5 4 3 2 1
BD666 – 06/09

All rights reserved under International and Pan-American Copyright Conventions. No part of this publication may be reproduced, stored in a retrieval system, or transmitted in any form or by any means, electronic, mechanical, photocopying, recording, or otherwise, without the prior written permission of the copyright owner. Published in Great Britain by Dorling Kindersley Limited.

A Cataloging-in-Publication record for this book is available from the Library of Congress.

ISBN: 978-0-7566-5587-7

Printed and bound by
Leo Paper Products, China

Discover more at
www.dk.com

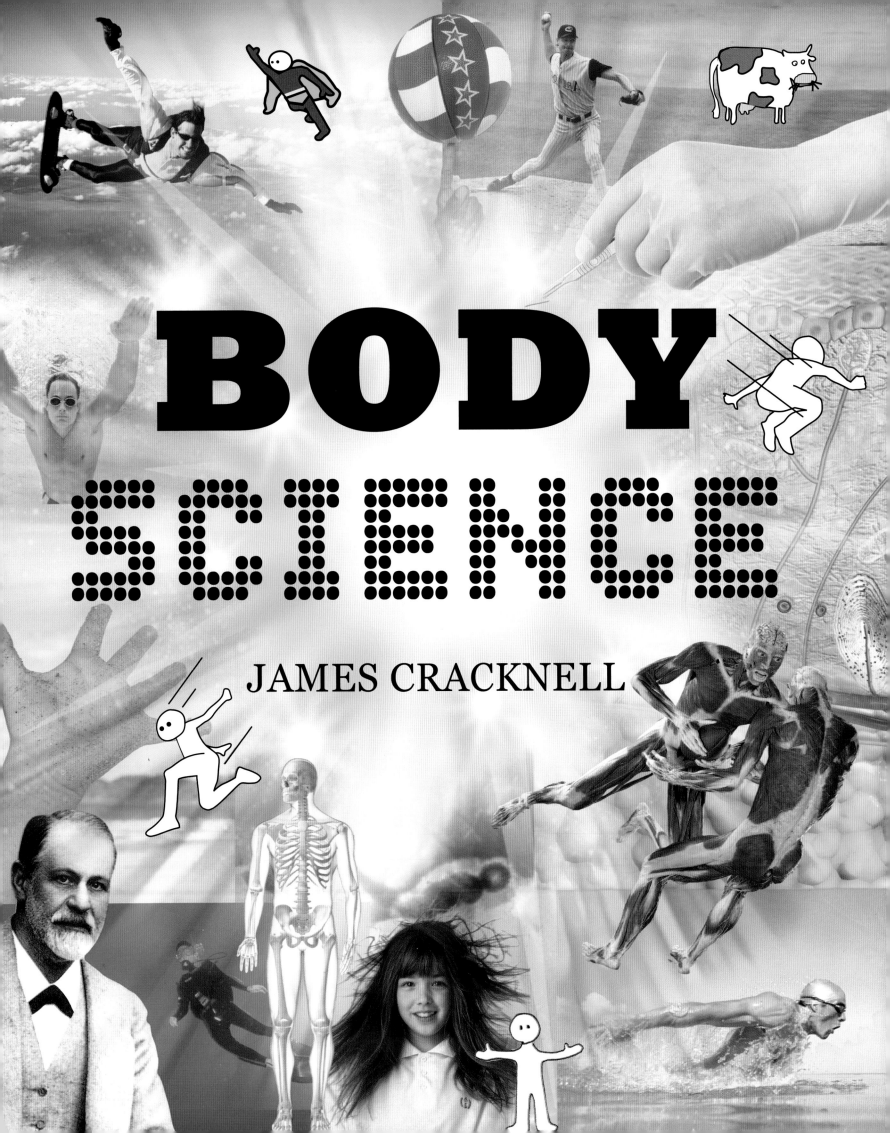

BODY SCIENCE

JAMES CRACKNELL

Contents

1 Energy

2 Control

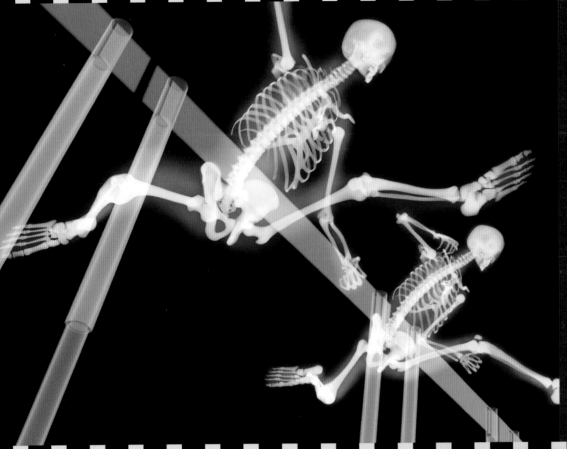

Introduction

If you could own the most amazing machine in the world, what would it be? The latest James Bond car, the Space Shuttle, a jet fighter, a submarine, or maybe a supercomputer? The thing is, each of us already has it—our own body.

The human body achieves feats other machines can only dream about (if they could dream, that is...). We've climbed Mount Everest, run at over 27 mph (43.5 km/h), and dived more than 650 ft (200 m) below the sea. We can survive in both the Sahara Desert and tropical rain forests; the human body has conquered the North and South poles; it can fight disease and even heal itself. We may not be able to fly, but using our own supercomputer—the brain—we have managed to build machines that can fly for us and even take us to the Moon.

But despite being supermachines, we are still under the control of scientific principles, and not just biological ones. The very reason we can't fly (or even jump as high as we would like) is because of Earth's forces, or more specifically in this case, gravity. At times we have to admit defeat to these factors. That's hardly surprising since humans are so new to Earth—we're still babies compared to the earliest forms of life, which have been around for 4,000,000,000 years.

Science affects our bodies all of the time. We are basically a living experiment. Everything that affects Earth impacts on our bodies, and we can learn so much about ourselves from the world around us. Without the life-giving energy of the Sun and water, to the gases in the air that we need to breathe, neither our planet nor our bodies would work.

Understanding how your body works is a huge subject, but in this book we've broken it up into small chunks that are easy to understand. There are no boring biology diagrams! Instead, everything is explained in a clear, fun, and interesting way with plenty of great examples. I promise that every time you turn a page there'll be a fact about the body that will shock or surprise you. You will start to realize how amazing your body is. In fact, we are living supermen and women: our bones are stronger than concrete, they store all the harmful metals that can poison us, and if we break a bone they fuse back together stronger than before. Incredible.

We'll take you through the basics of which bone goes where and how body parts connect, but you will also learn how and why your body reacts as it does in different situations. At the start of the Olympics I felt nervous, and as a response my brain instructed my nervous system to help out by releasing epinephrine (aka adrenaline). My breathing rate increased to raise oxygen levels in my blood, oxygen and glucose (energy) went to the muscles and brain, and endorphins were increased to dull the pain; my body was ready for anything. All this happened because I was nervous.

We also explore the science of extreme activities, how training can lead to some freaky bodies, and look into the future of body science by examining forensics, bionics, rebuilding body parts, and cloning.

Most importantly, enjoy and look after your amazing machine. We hope this book will make you understand and appreciate it even more and how it fits into the world.

James Cracknell

Energy is everywhere. **Without it nothing would work.** The lights wouldn't come on in the morning, the shower wouldn't work, and don't even think about making toast.

To most of us, energy is what powers the gizmos and gadgets that make life easier. But it is also vital for life. Your body is a machine, and to live, move, and grow it needs energy.

Like fuel running a power plant, food gives you the energy to do stuff. But where did food get its energy?

In the following pages, we'll take a look at energy, where it comes from, and how the body uses it as a currency to get things done...

Energy

Life on EARTH in a YEAR

Humans have only been around for a blink of an eye. Scientists think the Earth is 4.6 billion years old and that life has only been around for about 4 billion years. All these billions of years can be confusing...

1 January

No life. Earth is a barren, lifeless chunk of space rock.

4.6 billion years ago...

FEBRUARY 14

The earliest form of life appears—simple cells known as **prokaryotes**.

3.8 billion years ago...

MARCH 2

Cells start to use sunlight to make energy—a process called **photosynthesis**.

3.6 billion years ago...

MAY 30

More complex cells called **eukaryotes** start to appear.

2.7 billion years ago...

NOVEMBER 16

Primitive **invertebrates** scuttle along the ocean floor.

550 million years ago...

NOVEMBER 20

The large oceans start to house **fish and coral**.

500 million years ago...

NOVEMBER 25

The first mosslike **land plants** start to grow on the rocky surface.

430 million years ago...

NOVEMBER 28

Insects appear—first walking on land and then flying in the air.

410 million years ago...

DECEMBER 14

The first **mammals** start to roam the land.

210 million years ago...

DECEMBER 18

The skies are full of **birds** and **plants flower** for the first time.

150 million years ago...

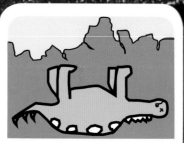

DECEMBER 25

The **dinosaurs** bow out from the theater of life. Was it a meteor or disease?

65 million years ago...

DECEMBER 31

7:09 p.m. The first in the **genus of** *Homo* (early humans) walk on Earth.

2.5 million years ago...

... so let's take a look at the evolution of life as if it all happened in a year.

JULY 8

The first signs of **multicellular life** in the form of marine algae evolves.

1.7 million years ago...

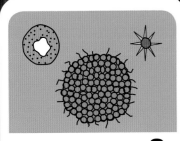

DECEMBER 3

Animals crawl from the sea and the **first amphibians** evolve.

360 million years ago...

DECEMBER 31

11:36 p.m. **Humans** start to look like we do today.

250,000 years ago...

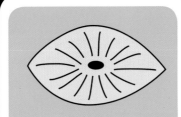

NOVEMBER 14

The first jelly-bodied **marine ancestors** of animals are born.

630 million years ago...

DECEMBER 7

The first land-only **reptiles** are born.

290 million years ago...

DECEMBER 31

11:57 p.m. **Neanderthals**, the last of our early human relatives, die out.

25,000 years ago...

Science discoveries COUNTDOWN

Wow! A lot has happened in a year. But it's not until the last 20 seconds that science really gets going. As the new year looms, here's a countdown of scientific discoveries!

20 seconds to go...

Anaximander thinks Earth is curved and floats in space (**550 BCE**)

Greek geeks consider the nature of matter (**450 BCE**)

Archimedes takes a bath and discovers water forces (**250 BCE**)

The Greeks measure the size of Earth using shadows (**240 BCE**)

10 seconds to go...

Persian scientist Alhazen writes the first book on optics (**1000 CE**)

The Chinese know the way and invent the compass (**1040**)

Grosseteste pioneers the value of scientific method (**1215**)

05 seconds to go...

Copernicus argues that Earth revolves around the Sun (**1543**)

Robert Boyle starts a discussion of chemical elements (**1661**)

Newton writes his laws of motion (**1687**)

Franklin uses a kite to prove lightning is electricity (**1752**)

Cavendish proves water isn't an element (**1784**)

Thomas Young enlightens us about light waves (**1803**)

01 second to go...

Darwin and Wallace write about the evolution of species (**1858**)

Pasteur proposes the germ theory of disease (**1861**)

Mendeleev draws up the periodic table (**1869**)

Lord Rayleigh explains why the sky is blue (**1871**)

Roentgen discovers X-rays (**1895**)

Landsteiner figures out basic blood groups (**1902**)

Albert Einstein publishes first paper on relativity (**1905**)

Tom Morgan discusses heredity and chromosomes (**1926**)

Lemaitre coins the Big Bang Theory (**1927**)

Programmable computers invented (**1943**)

The first nuclear bomb dropped on Hiroshima (**1945**)

DNA's double helix unraveled (**1953**)

One small step for man: first men on the Moon (**1969**)

Oh, Dolly! The first mammal (sheep) is cloned (**1996**)

The worldwide web moves into our homes (**1998**)

The human genome is deciphered (**2003**)

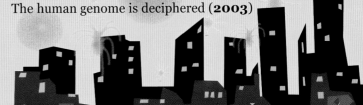

SOLAR POWER

The Sun is 93 million miles (150 million kilometers) away from Earth.

Solar power sounds like a recent invention, but it's not. It has been around since the dawn of time and almost every living thing on Earth is powered by it.

The Sun is a big ball of burning hydrogen gas. The temperature at the center of the Sun reaches over **18,000,000°F (10,000,000°C)!** This high temperature combined with the high pressure causes millions of nuclear reactions to take place.

SUNSHINE POWER PLANT

The Sun is the energy factory of Earth. Every second the Sun produces about 5 million tons of pure energy. This travels out into space as sunlight. Some of it reaches Earth and it is this sunlight energy that is trapped by plants and used as fuel. Humans are unable to convert sunlight energy directly. We aren't solar powered; instead, we need it changed into an energy we can use. A little like finding the right-shaped battery for your favorite toy, humans need the right type of energy to work—**chemical energy**.

The Earth's atmosphere reduces the intensity of the Sun's rays. The sunlight that gets through is ready to be converted into usable energy.

LIGHT ENERGY

How is sunlight converted into chemical energy?

A brilliant process called **photosynthesis** allows plants to absorb the sunlight and change it into chemical energy, which is then used by the plants.

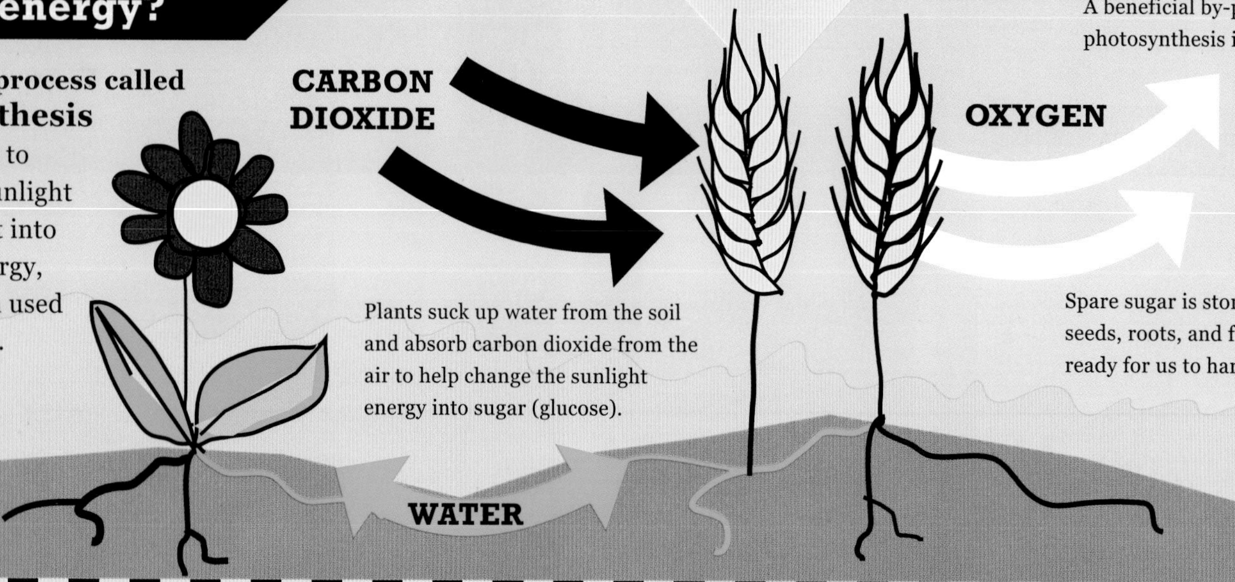

CARBON DIOXIDE

A beneficial by-product of photosynthesis is oxygen.

OXYGEN

Plants suck up water from the soil and absorb carbon dioxide from the air to help change the sunlight energy into sugar (glucose).

Spare sugar is stored in seeds, roots, and fruits, ready for us to harvest.

WATER

water + carbon dioxide + sunlight = oxygen + chemical energy

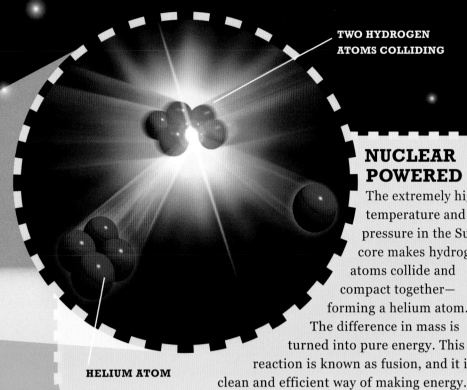

TWO HYDROGEN ATOMS COLLIDING

HELIUM ATOM

NUCLEAR POWERED

The extremely high temperature and pressure in the Sun's core makes hydrogen atoms collide and compact together— forming a helium atom. The difference in mass is turned into pure energy. This reaction is known as fusion, and it is a clean and efficient way of making energy.

Sunlight takes 8½ minutes to reach Earth. It travels at the speed of light, 186,282 mile/s (299,792 km/s).

HOME ENERGY Most of the electricity you use at home is made by the Sun. Large power plants are fueled by *fossil fuels*, which are the remains of plants that once, millions of years ago, trapped the Sun's energy.

RENEWABLE ENERGY Fossil fuels won't last forever and are polluting the atmosphere. So, scientists are spending more time looking for renewable sources of energy. Solar panels and wind turbines use the Sun's rays and its influence on our weather to make energy (and they are less polluting, too).

Humans have learned to combine different plants to make new foods, like bread, cakes, and candies. Eating plants isn't the only way humans absorb chemical energy. Humans are also meat eaters and we absorb the Sun's energy by eating animals that have eaten plants.

I spend a quarter of the day munching on grass and my four stomachs help me absorb the chemical energy.

Humans need energy to survive, from breathing and thinking, to moving and eating. We need oxygen to help turn stored chemical energy into movement (kinetic energy).

CHEMICAL ENERGY

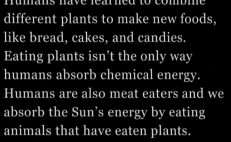

KINETIC ENERGY

chemical energy + water = carbon dioxide + water + kinetic energy

ENERGY makes the body go round

Energy is used to get stuff done. The body wouldn't be able to do anything without it. So how does energy get work done? Well, the best way to see energy is as a currency. Like money makes the world go round, energy does the same to your body.

THE BODY BANK
Once you have eaten your energy, it gets stored around your body, like savings in a bank. Unless you release it, it just sits there and doesn't do anything. These savings are usually in the form of chemical energy.

Energy has the amazing talent of being indestructible. It never disappears, it just changes form, like money changing hands.

INVESTMENT
eating food stores chemical energy

The food we eat contains chemical energy and that is the perfect energy type to make our bodies work. By eating food we are *investing* energy into our bodies, like putting *savings* into the bank. Any chemical energy we don't use is stored for future activities, when it can be exchanged into different energy currencies.

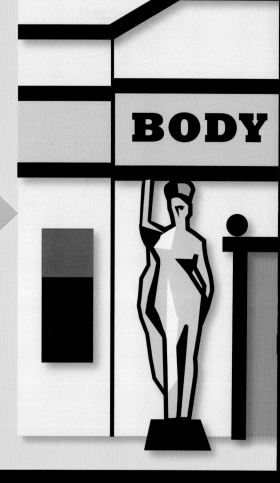

BODY

ENERGY CURRENCIES
There are different types of energy—similar to the different currencies you get around the world. You can change money from one currency to another when you need it for your vacations. Energy acts in the same way.

Electrical energy is a very fast and efficient type of energy. Our brain and nerves use a type of electrical energy to get messages around the body.

Heat energy is generated by particles moving. The faster they move the hotter they get. In the body heat is normally a by-product of energy conversion.

Kinetic energy is the energy of movement. The faster something moves the more kinetic energy it has. The body changes chemical energy into kinetic movement.

THE BODY BANK ACCOUNTS

There are two different energy bank accounts in your body. They both allow access to your invested energy, but offer different ways of getting your hands on it. Your body uses both energy bank accounts for different types of activities.

AEROBIC

The **aerobic** account is for the **patient** and **steady investor**. It has a slower release of energy and needs oxygen, but it gives you more for your money, allowing you to *keep going for longer*.

ANAEROBIC

The **anaerobic** account is for the **quick** and **explosive shopper**. They want their energy quickly, but unfortunately, it doesn't go very far and only supplies energy for *short periods of time*.

BANK

SPENDING
physical activity uses kinetic energy

The body has a lot of work to do. From the brain thinking, the lungs breathing, and to the heart pumping—they all need energy. Then on top of that there's all the physical activity we like to do. Luckily, we don't have to feed ourselves as we work; instead, the body draws on the chemical savings that have been invested and converts them into kinetic energy. The exchange isn't 100 percent perfect because some energy is changed into heat energy.

chemical

Chemical energy is the energy trapped in molecules. Most plants use photosynthesis to trap this energy. Food and gasoline are high in chemical energy.

LIGHT

Light energy is made in stars, like our Sun. It moves at amazing speeds and can travel vast distances. Unfortunately, the body can't process it directly.

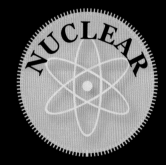

NUCLEAR

Nuclear energy is made when minute particles, atoms, are split or fused. It produces lots of energy. The body doesn't use this form of energy.

CASH ENERGY The chemical investments stored in the body are used by the body's cells to do their work. For this, the cells need the chemical energy to be turned into a currency they can use. Instead of using a cash machine to take energy out as cash, they use *cellular respiration*, which converts stored chemical energy into ATP (adenosine triphosphate)—the raw energy used by every cell.

Body MATTER

Matter is all around you. Everything is made of it. Matter consists of three main states—**solid, liquid, and gas**. Each state of matter is influenced by energy and acts differently. These properties make them suited to different roles in the body.

The human body is made up of each state of matter—solid, liquid, and gas. They all work together to make the body run smoothly, like a finely tuned machine.

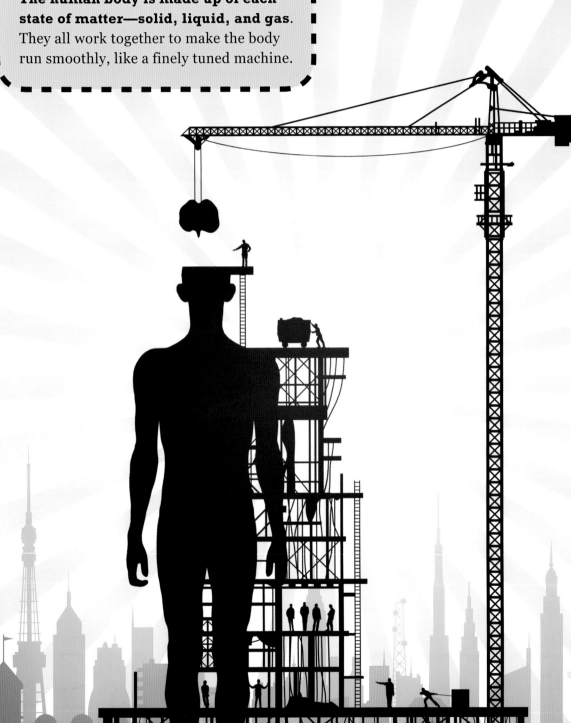

The particles in solids are packed closely together. They have little energy and this keeps them compact and strong.

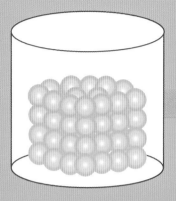

Liquid particles have more energy and flow easily over each other. Liquids take the shape of the container they are in.

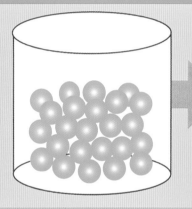

Gas particles have even more energy and are even farther apart. All they want to do is escape.

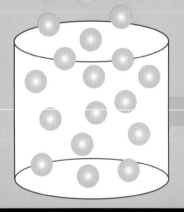

There is a 4th STATE OF MATTER...

solid

Most solids are hard, like teeth and bone, though some can be soft, like the heart and brain. Solids have a fixed volume and can hold their shape without any support, but most can be chipped, snapped, or cut.

Matter has different properties in different states. The state matter takes is dependent on energy. Matter switches between states by removing or adding energy, normally heat.

When a liquid cools down its particles lose their energy and they slow down, becoming less fluid and more **solid**.

FREEZE

MELT

liquid

Liquids are fluid and want to flow away. Though liquids can change their shape, their volume remains the same. Some liquids flow more easily than others; this is known as viscosity. Blood, for example, is more viscous (thicker) than water.

When solids heat up, they gain more energy and their particles break their bonds and become **liquid**.

When gas loses energy it slows down and its particles stick together, becoming **liquid**.

CONDENSE

EVAPORATE

gas

Gases want to expand and drift away. Their shape and volume is constantly changing, depending on the space they are in. You breathe gases in and out of your lungs and they are carried around your body by the blood.

When a liquid heats up it gains energy and its particles start to move farther apart, until they are whizzing around as **gas particles**.

plasma

Plasma is a gas and is formed at extremely high temperatures. The Sun makes a natural plasma, but plasmas can also be created artificially for use in television screens and fluorescent light bulbs. Plasma gas acts differently to normal gases because it is influenced by electric and magnetic fields. Part of the blood is also called

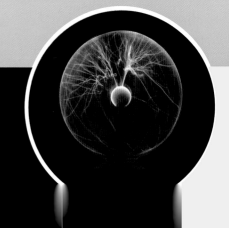

It's a GAS BUSINESS

Gas and energy go hand in hand. Without gas, humans would struggle to survive. This is because gas is what we breathe. And **breathing is vital to life**. But why is this? Well, believe it or not, most of the energy in our bodies is useless. It is chemical energy that we have absorbed from food. But this energy is trapped. To release it, we need oxygen, and we need it in our bloodstream NOW! Here's how it gets there.

It all happens in THE LUNG FACTORY
Swim with me to the factory. And then you'll see.

Your lungs' surface area is the size of a tennis court.

You breathe in and out around 20 times a minute.

A GOOD THING about gas is that it moves and diffuses at great speed. This means it positively races to your cells, where it helps make your body's energy. Just imagine if you breathed solids or liquids. Their slower particles would takes ages to reach the cells. This would make you very sluggish—unlike gas breathers who can run at high speed!

Air breathed measured in liters per minute

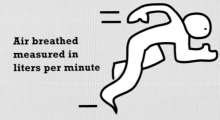

High intensity RUNNING—150 L/min

MARATHON RUNNING—90 L/min

SITTING— 6 L/min

Lungs are like a non-stop factory.

78% nitrogen 21% oxygen

Take a breath
The average person breathes in 6 liters of fresh air a minute. But not all of that is oxygen! The air we breathe is a mixture of gases. The main two are oxygen and nitrogen.

You breathe air into your lungs through your nose and mouth.

CO2 oxygen

Lungs

You have two lungs, one on each side of your chest. On the outside, they are pink and squishy, but inside they are packed with tiny airways, which branch out like trees.

Capillaries

Alveoli

WHERE THE GAS GOES
At the ends of the airways are around 600 million tiny air sacs (called alveoli), and these are covered in even tinier blood vessels (called capillaries). When you breathe in, the air sacs fill up with air. And when you breathe out, they empty out.

Blood O2
CO2 **Lungs**

GAS DIFFUSION
Once it's in the air sacs, oxygen (O2) pushes its way through the walls and into the bloodstream in a process called diffusion. At the same time carbon dioxide (CO2) diffuses back the other way—from the blood into the air sacs. You don't need the carbon dioxide, so you just breathe it out of your body!

THE GAS EXCHANGE
Gas can move from air to liquid (like oxygen from your lungs into your blood), or from liquid to gas (carbon dioxide traveling from your blood to your lungs). But how does this work? Well, when you breathe in, there is more oxygen in your lungs than in your blood. Oxygen doesn't seem to like this, so it travels into the blood in an effort to even things out. Carbon dioxide has the same sort of idea— there is more of it in the blood than the lungs, so it diffuses back into the lungs. It's a little like the carbon dioxide in a carbonated drink. There is far more carbon dioxide in the drink than in the air. So when you open the bottle, all the tiny bubbles of carbon dioxide race to get out!

A BODY OF WATER

Three-quarters of my body weight is due to water. That's heavy, man!

Water covers nearly three-quarters of the Earth. **Our bodies are about 60 percent water**. It really is water, water everywhere. Water, like sunlight, is vital to almost all life on Earth, but what does it do? Let's have a look at how this amazing liquid gives us a thirst for life.

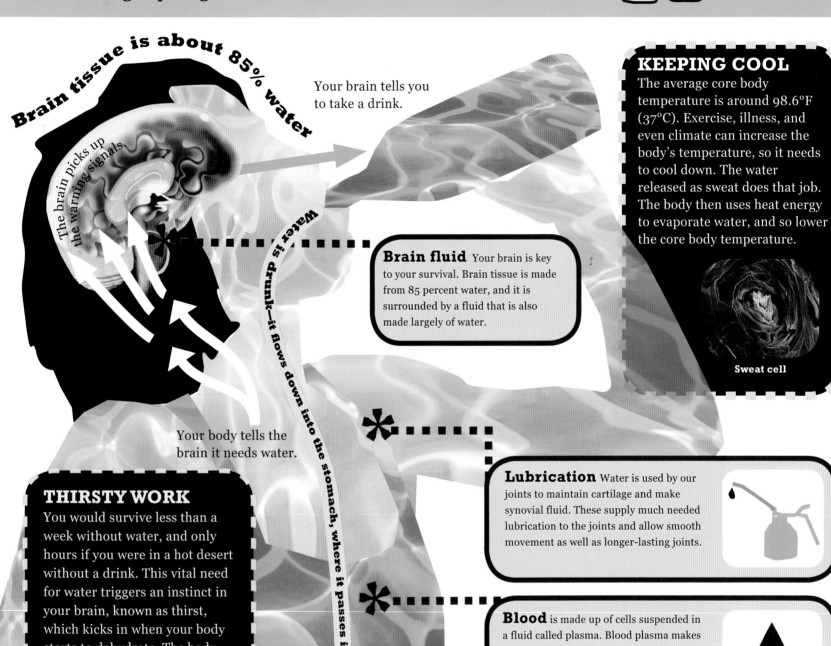

Brain tissue is about 85% water

Your brain tells you to take a drink.

The brain picks up the warning signals.

Water is drunk—it flows down into the stomach, where it passes into the rest of the body.

Your body tells the brain it needs water.

Brain fluid Your brain is key to your survival. Brain tissue is made from 85 percent water, and it is surrounded by a fluid that is also made largely of water.

KEEPING COOL

The average core body temperature is around 98.6°F (37°C). Exercise, illness, and even climate can increase the body's temperature, so it needs to cool down. The water released as sweat does that job. The body then uses heat energy to evaporate water, and so lower the core body temperature.

Sweat cell

THIRSTY WORK

You would survive less than a week without water, and only hours if you were in a hot desert without a drink. This vital need for water triggers an instinct in your brain, known as thirst, which kicks in when your body starts to dehydrate. The body steals water from less vital tissues and fluids, such as saliva; that makes your mouth feel dry. Sensors throughout the body keep a check on water levels and tell the brain when you need more water.

Lubrication Water is used by our joints to maintain cartilage and make synovial fluid. These supply much needed lubrication to the joints and allow smooth movement as well as longer-lasting joints.

Blood is made up of cells suspended in a fluid called plasma. Blood plasma makes up about 55 percent of blood and is mostly water. The body needs water to maintain a consistent volume of blood, around 5 liters (10½ pints).

Energy Water is vital in the production of the raw energy produced and used by the body's cells. Water is also needed to make the gastric juices that help break down food ready for energy production.

Rehydration

Replacing the water your body uses, especially after exercise, is very important. Many sports drinks also contain sodium and potassium salts, which are lost through sweating. These help your nerve cells to work as they should.

80% water
20% juice

Isotonic

These are good for replacing fluids fast. They contain 20 percent fruit juice, which gives the body a sugar boost, replacing some of the energy that has been lost.

90% water
10% juice

Hypotonic

These offer fast fluid replacement and have a higher percentage of water. They don't give much of an energy boost and are best after exercise to prevent dehydration.

71% water
29% juice

Hypertonic

These offer more energy replacement, with nearly a third of their mix made from sugary juice. This type of drink is best drunk after exercise to replenish lost energy.

Headaches When the body loses water, doing stuff becomes harder and you get tired. If your brain doesn't get enough water, it produces chemicals that cause pain, alerting you to the problem.

Sweating and breathing are two ways we lose water from the body. Exercise and hot weather make you sweat much faster.

Blood is mostly water, and when the amount of water in the blood drops, it affects the rest of your body. With less water present, the volume of blood decreases, and your heart has to work harder to pump it around the body. If the brain and other organs don't receive enough blood they can't work correctly, and you start to feel weak and confused.

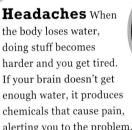

During vigorous exercise we sweat around 2 pints per hour.

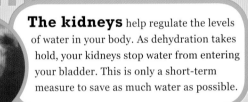

The kidneys help regulate the levels of water in your body. As dehydration takes hold, your kidneys stop water from entering your bladder. This is only a short-term measure to save as much water as possible.

RUNNING ON EMPTY

All the water in the body has substances dissolved in it. Every living cell needs water, and the process by which water moves in and out of the cells is called osmosis. Water will move across a cell wall if there is less water on the other side, so as to keep the solution inside and outside the cell at the same concentration. If you start to dehydrate, water is drawn out of the cells to keep the amount of water in the blood at the right level. As little as a 2 percent drop in body water can lead to symptoms of dehydration.

Cramps If you are exercising hard you may start to get cramp in your muscles as they lose water and salts.

TOO MUCH WATER Even though it is important to keep hydrated, you can overdo it. Drinking too much plain water can upset the delicate balance between water and dissolved salts in the body. If the salts become too diluted, the brain starts to swell, which can be dangerous.

Solid SUPERHERO

Bones are **lightweight and strong** and are **ideal for moving.** Imagine trying to walk with heavy bones!

Bones are **tough** and **provide protection** to major organs—most importantly the brain.

Bones have a small amount of elasticity and absorb some of the impact from moving.

Our bodies might contain liquids and gases, but as a whole we are **solid beings**. Solids have many properties that make them ideal for certain roles in the body. Some of these properties are truly amazing, like superpowers. So, let's check out *solids* and your *inner superhero*.

SOLID PROPERTIES

Hardness
This is how resistant solids are to being dented or scratched.

Density
This is how much matter (atoms or molecules) is packed into the object's volume.

Elasticity
This is the ability to return to an original state after being stretched.

Mild-mannered SKELETON
Superman uses Clark Kent, Batman has Bruce Wayne, and Wonder Woman is Diana Prince. So who is the alter ego of your solid superhero? Well, it's the skeleton. The skeleton is a collection of solids, most notably the bones. On the surface it doesn't look like much, but there's more to it than meets the eye socket...

The skeleton offers a solid framework for muscles to attach.

vertebrae

The spine is made up of 33 small bones called vertebrae. They sit on top of each other, separated by cushioning disks. The spine provides amazing flexibility and strength.

spongy bone

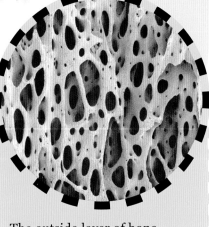

The outside layer of bone is tough and compact. Inside is what is known as spongy bone, which is a mix of bone and air. This gives spongy bone a low density, making it light but also very strong.

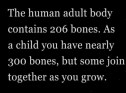

The human adult body contains 206 bones. As a child you have nearly 300 bones, but some join together as you grow.

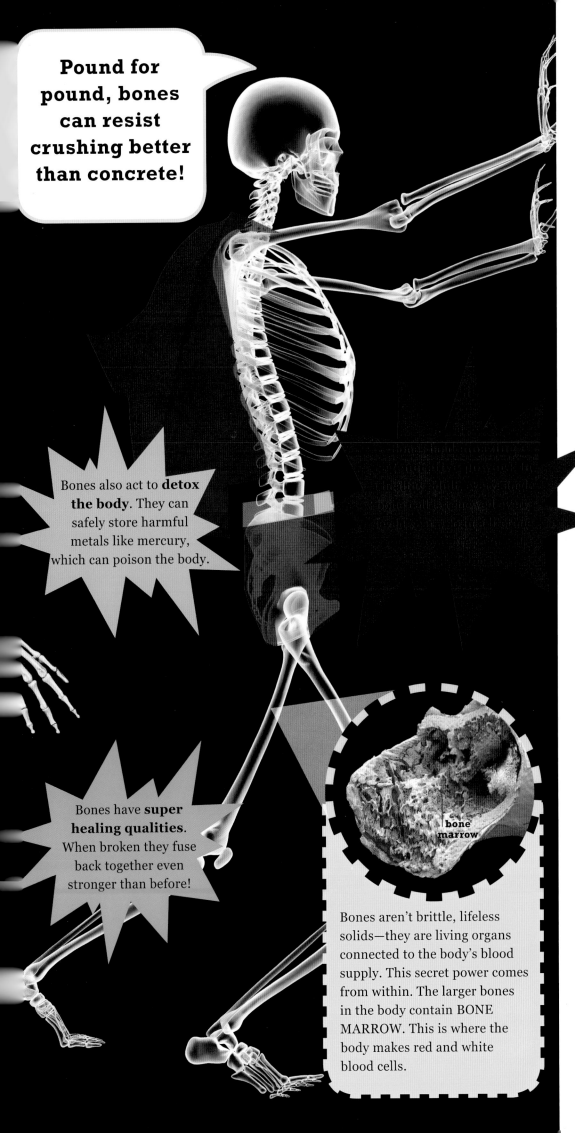

> **Pound for pound, bones can resist crushing better than concrete!**

Bones also act to **detox the body**. They can safely store harmful metals like mercury, which can poison the body.

Bones have **super healing qualities**. When broken they fuse back together even stronger than before!

bone marrow

Bones aren't brittle, lifeless solids—they are living organs connected to the body's blood supply. This secret power comes from within. The larger bones in the body contain BONE MARROW. This is where the body makes red and white blood cells.

All good superheroes have a SIDEKICK

The skeleton can't perform all the solid roles the body demands. It is given a helping hand from some other dynamic solids.

Teeth

Their hard edges help to mash and cut food—vital for taking in the energy we need to survive.

Nails

Your fingernails might look useless, but think again. Try untying a knot without them!

Ligaments, cartilage, muscles

These tissues all attach, support, and move the skeleton. Their properties make them perfect sidekicks. Their main power is in their high elasticity, which helps absorb, stabilize, and control impact and movement.

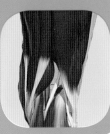

Skin tights and underpants

Your skin is the body's largest organ. It protects and guards the body from the outside world and stretches over your unique body shape. On top of its protective qualities, skin is waterproof, helps to maintain body temperature, makes vitamin D from the Sun's rays, and gives us the ability to feel and touch. The skin can also mend itself—when broken or cut, it heals by forming a protective cap, known as a scab. A true super suit!

Little bits of Body

Making a body isn't as simple as pouring the right measurements of elements into a mixer and spinning everything around. The architecture of our bodies is fantastically complex, from systems, organs, and cells, right down to the tiniest building blocks of all—atoms.

ATOMS

These are generally considered the smallest building blocks, but atoms themselves are made from even smaller parts, called subatomic particles, meaning smaller than an atom. An atom has a nucleus made of protons (red, below) and neutrons (green). Protons have a positive electrical charge, and neutrons are neutral. The third subatomic particle is the electron (yellow). Electrons are little balls of negatively charged energy that orbit the central nucleus. Atoms of a particular element (or basic type) always have the same number of protons. This number gives an element its unique atomic number.

Proton
Neutron
Electron

SIZE MATTERS
If an atom is minuscule, how small is its nucleus? Well, if you think of the nucleus as the size of a golf ball, then the atom itself would be the size of the Eiffel Tower!

EACH CHEMICAL element is made up of its own type of atom. Millions of these tiny particles join together to make the element. So, calcium is only made from calcium atoms and hydrogen is only made from hydrogen atoms.

TYPES OF CELLS in the human body

BLOOD CELLS make up nearly half the cells in your body. Red blood cells carry oxygen to the body's tissues and carry away waste (carbon dioxide). White blood cells fight infection.

EYE CELLS include rod cells and cone cells at the back of the eye, which help you see color and tones. Lens cells (shown here), help to focus light on the back of the eye to make clear images.

NERVE CELLS are called neurons, and their job is to carry messages to and from your brain. The messages travel as electrical signals and tell your heart to beat, legs to walk, and fingers to feel.

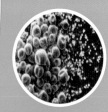

FAT CELLS mostly occur just under our skin. They look a little like oil-filled bubbles and are where our bodies store excess energy from the food we eat. Fat cells increase in number as we get fatter.

BRAIN CELLS include neurons and glial cells. There are 100 billion neurons in the brain and even more glial cells. Glial cells are support cells—their job is to help neurons work effectively.

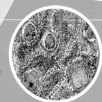

SKIN CELLS form under the surface of your skin, then move up over the next month. Around 30,000 skins cells flake off every day—and these make up most of the dust in your home!

ATOMS make ELEMENTS, which make our BODY CELLS!

ORGANS

The main players in the business of the body are the organs. Here are a few of the key members.

HEART This is the body's blood pump. It sends blood to the lungs, and pumps it around the whole body.

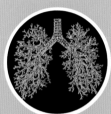

LUNGS These are where oxygen passes into the blood, and carbon dioxide passes out of it. Lungs fill with gas (and empty out) about 20 times a minute.

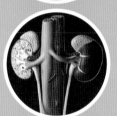

KIDNEYS These two organs are the cleaners of the body. They filter out waste chemicals and excess liquid, and turn them into urine.

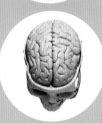

BRAIN This is the nerve center of the body. It controls actions like breathing and allows us to think. The brain is as soft as pudding, so is protected by the hard bone of the skull.

SKIN The largest organ in the body, the skin acts as a protective barrier against the outside world. It is packed with nerves and senses touch or pain.

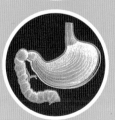

STOMACH This is where your food goes when you swallow it. Your stomach partially digests your food, churning it into a thick liquid called chyme.

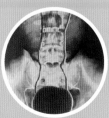

BLADDER The body produces a lot of liquid waste, and this is the holding area. When it's full of urine, you need to go!

CELLS join together to make ORGANS

BODY SYSTEMS

Organs work in teams, known as systems. There are seven major body systems with seven different functions, all make one working human.

ENDOCRINE SYSTEM This sends chemical messages, called hormones, around the body to control sleep, temperature, growth, and reproduction.

RESPIRATORY SYSTEM
The most important part of this system is the lungs. They take in air, so oxygen can pass into the blood system. And they remove waste carbon dioxide.

DIGESTIVE SYSTEM
This is pretty much one long tube from your mouth to your you-know-what! Everything you eat passes through here.

CIRCULATORY SYSTEM
This is your heart and blood vessels. Blood carries oxygen and nutrients around the body, and carries away carbon dioxide.

NERVOUS SYSTEM This, the body's information network, comprises the brain and nerves. It works at lightning speeds—signals zip along nerves at 250 mph (400 km/h).

MUSCLES There are two kinds—voluntary muscles that you use when you turn your head, and involuntary muscles that work without you thinking about them, such as when your heart beats.

BONES These give your body shape and hold it upright. Bones are living tissue, with spaces for blood vessels and nerves. If you cut them, they bleed, and if you break them, they grow back together again.

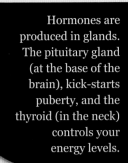

Hormones are produced in glands. The pituitary gland (at the base of the brain), kick-starts puberty, and the thyroid (in the neck) controls your energy levels.

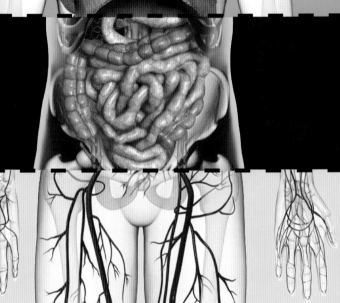

Chemical CREATION

So we know that matter makes up everything **around us,** and that it has different states, making our bodies work efficiently. ***But what is matter?*** Matter is a general name for all the substances in the universe. **Wood**, **air**, **metal**, even your skin and bones, can be broken down into simpler substances called **ELEMENTS.**

H HYDROGEN 1																		He HELIUM 2
Li LITHIUM 3	Be BERYLLIUM 4											B BORON 5	C CARBON 6	N NITROGEN 7	O OXYGEN 8	F 9	Ne NEON 10
Na SODIUM 11	Mg MAGNESIUM 12											Al Aluminum 13	Si SILICON 14	P PHOSPHORUS 15	S SULFUR 16	Cl 17	Ar ARGON 18
K POTASSIUM 19	Ca CALCIUM 20	Sc SCANDIUM 21	Ti TITANIUM 22	V VANADIUM 23	Cr CHROMIUM 24	Mn MANGANESE 25	Fe IRON 26	Co COBALT 27	Ni NICKEL 28	Cu COPPER 29	Zn ZINC 30	Ga GALLIUM 31	Ge GERMANIUM 32	As ARSENIC 33	Se SELENIUM 34	Br 35	Kr KRYPTON 36
Rb RUBIDIUM 37	Sr STRONTIUM 38	Y YTTRIUM 39	Zr ZIRCONIUM 40	Nb NIOBIUM 41	Mo MOLYBDENUM 42	Tc TECHNETIUM 43	Ru RUTHENIUM 44	Rh RHODIUM 45	Pd PALLADIUM 46	Ag SILVER 47	Cd CADMIUM 48	In INDIUM 49	Sn TIN 50	Sb ANTIMONY 51	Te TELLURIUM 52	I 53	Xe XENON 54
Cs Cesium 55	Ba BARIUM 56	LANTHANIDES or RARE-EARTH METALS 57—71	Hf HAFNIUM 72	Ta TANTALUM 73	W TUNGSTEN 74	Re RHENIUM 75	Os OSMIUM 76	Ir IRIDIUM 77	Pt PLATINUM 78	Au GOLD 79	Hg MERCURY 80	Tl THALLIUM 81	Pb LEAD 82	Bi BISMUTH 83	Po POLONIUM 84	At 85	Rn RADON 86
Fr FRANCIUM 87	Ra RADIUM 88	ACTINIDES or RARE-EARTH RADIOACTIVE METALS 89—103	Rf RUTHERFORDIUM 104	Db DUBNIUM 105	Sg SEABORGIUM 106	Bh BOHRIUM 107	Hs HASSIUM 108	Mt MEITNERIUM 109	Ds DARMSTADTIUM 110	Rg ROENTGENIUM 111							

Each vertical column is called a GROUP, or family, of elements. Some groups have elements sharing very similar properties. Other groups have elements with less in common.

La LANTHANUM 57	Ce CERIUM 58	Pr PRASEODYMIUM 59	Nd NEODYMIUM 60	Pm PROMETHIUM 61	Sm SAMARIUM 62	Eu EUROPIUM 63	Gd GADOLINIUM 64	Tb TERBIUM 65	Dy DYSPROSIUM 66	Ho HOLMIUM 67	Er ERBIUM 68	Tm THULIUM 69	Yb YTTERBIUM 70	Lu LUTETIUM 71
Ac ACTINIUM 89	Th THORIUM 90	Pa PROTACTINIUM 91	U URANIUM 92	Np NEPTUNIUM 93	Pu PLUTONIUM 94	Am AMERICIUM 95	Cm CURIUM 96	Bk BERKELIUM 97	Cf CALIFORNIUM 98	Es EINSTEINIUM 99	Fm FERMIUM 100	Md MENDELEVIUM 101	No NOBELIUM 102	Lr LAWRENCIUM 103

*

Dmitri Mendeleev was a Russian scientist who devised this version of the periodic table, which enabled other scientists to include new elements as they were discovered.

The periodic table

is a way of displaying the 111 known elements. All the elements are listed in order of increasing atomic number. Atomic numbers are based on the number of protons in the nucleus of an atom. The way they are arranged relates to the properties of the element. Scientists noted that some elements had similar properties according to the number and arrangement of the electrons in the atom's outer shell. This enabled them to put them into vertical columns called groups and horizontal rows, or periods. Elements in groups react in a similar manner and form compounds the same way.

Element types

Elements can be grouped into similar types. Every element has a name, a symbol of one or two letters, and an atomic number.

Kr —— Symbol

KRYPTON —— Name

36 —— Atomic number

KEY:

- **Alkali metals:** *These silvery metals are very reactive.*
- **Alkaline-earth metals:** *These shiny, silvery-white metals are reactive.*
- **Transition metals:** *Many are strong and have high boiling and melting points.*
- **Lanthanides:** *Many are soft, shiny, and silvery-white metals.*
- **Actinides:** *These are radioactive heavy elements.*
- **Poor metals:** *Softer, weaker metals.*
- **Nonmetals:** *Most are gases at room temperature and easily snap as solids.*
- **Halogens:** *These nonmetals are highly reactive and harmful.*
- **Noble gases:** *These nonmetals are the least reactive of all the elements.*

O

OXYGEN

8

Oxygen is the most abundant element in the body, mainly in the form of water, H_2O.

C

CARBON

6

Carbon forms the basis of the body's most complex molecules, such as proteins.

H

HYDROGEN

1

Hydrogen is found in water molecules but is also important in making ATP.

N

NITROGEN

7

Nitrogen occurs in proteins and other organic compounds, and is the main gas in the atmosphere.

P

PHOSPHORUS

15

Phosphorus is vital in the formation of teeth and bones, and also the energy chemical ATP.

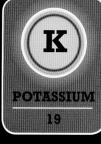

K

POTASSIUM

19

Potassium is a key chemical in making nerve cells transmit electrical signals.

Cl

CHLORINE

17

Chlorine is usually combined with sodium as salt. It is used for respiration and kidney function.

Na

SODIUM

11

Sodium controls the flow of water in the body and works with potassium in firing nerve cells.

Mg

MAGNESIUM

12

Magnesium helps the immune system to work, as well as the muscles and nerves.

S

SULFUR

16

Sulfur is vital in proteins, helps the blood to clot, and also makes your hair curl.

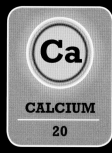

Ca

CALCIUM

20

Calcium makes the bones and teeth hard, and makes the heart and other muscles contract.

Fe

IRON

26

Iron is vital for carrying oxygen in the blood. It is found in meat and leafy vegetables.

I

IODINE

53

Iodine regulates many of the body's processes, such as digestion and hormones.

In addition to these 13, the body needs trace amounts of other elements, including copper, zinc, cobalt, lithium, fluorine, boron, chromium, and selenium.

10% hydrogen

65% oxygen (in H_2O)

0.15% chlorine

This is how much of each of the 13 ELEMENTS we're made of.

0.15% sodium

3% nitrogen

18% carbon

1% phosphorus

0.35% potassium

0.008% iron

1.6% calcium

0.25% sulfur

0.05% magnesium

0.00004% iodine

Not all of the elements are good for the body. Radioactive elements can kill cells.

There is a very strong acid in your body. Gastric juices contain hydrochloric acid, which breaks food down into smaller molecules during digestion.

The body also contains tiny amounts of poisonous elements, such as arsenic and mercury, but they are so small they don't cause any harm.

You are what YOU EAT

Your body is an amazing machine. But how does your body maintain and repair all its systems? Well, that's down to the fuel you put into your body. What you eat is vitally important because it has to contain everything that makes you you. Food doesn't just give you energy to do stuff, it also provides all the elements your body needs to grow and repair. To get the right elements **you have to eat a balanced diet containing the five main food groups**.

Carbohydrates

Fat

Carbo power

Carbohydrates are the body's main energy source. There are three main types—sugar, starch, and fiber. Carbohydrates are found in potatoes, rice, pasta, bread, and sugar. The body uses a sugar, called glucose, as fuel. Even though carbohydrates don't yield the most energy per gram, they are easy to access because they are stored in the blood, muscles, and liver.

Fuel Fill up your tank with carbs so you have the energy to work.

Digestion Fiber helps your body to digest and process food.

16 KJ **Energy** Carbo power only generates 16 kJ (3.8 kcal) per gram.

Fat at work

Too much fat isn't good for your body, but it does play a vital role. Fats help transport certain vitamins around the body in the bloodstream, like little taxis. They also help to build cell membranes and nerve cells. Fat does have the highest yield of energy per gram, however, it isn't used as a primary fuel source because the body is slower in turning it into usable energy.

Transportation Vitamins hitch a ride around the body on fat carriers.

Builder Fat is a key building material in the body.

37 KJ **Energy** Fat power generates an amazing 37 kJ (8.8 kcal) per gram.

A MEASURE OF ENERGY

Energy is measured in two ways—**kilojoules (kJ) and kilocalories (kcal)**. A kilojoule consists of 1,000 joules (J). A joule is the amount of energy needed to lift one kg one meter in the air. Kilocalories are normally refered to as calories, but scientifically they consist of 1,000 calories. A scientific calorie is the measure of energy needed to heat one gram of water by one degree Celsius. Both kilojoules and calories are used, but when you look at food labels or talk to people about food energy, you will mainly hear calories.

(1 kcal = 4.2 kJ)

READY... SET... GO!

1 Resting can actually be exhausting. It can burn up to **60 calories an hour**—that's nearly half a packet of potato chips.

2 No one likes doing chores, but did you know a little light housework can burn over **120 calories an hour!**

BODY BASICS

The body needs a basic level of energy to work. This is known as the Basal Metabolic Rate (BMR). This rate changes as you grow up and your body changes. Men usually have a higher BMR than women because they have more muscle, which needs more energy. As we enter old age our BMR decreases as body mass decreases. Also, the more active you are the more energy you'll need to eat.

Children should try to eat about 1,500 calories (kcals) a day to help them grow.

Men have a BMR of about 2,500 calories (kcals) a day.

Women have a BMR of about 2,000 calories (kcals) a day.

Protein

Vitamins

Vitamins The body needs four main vitamins—A, B, C, and D. Vitamins play an important role in building, protecting, and helping the body make energy. The body can make Vitamin D in the skin from sunlight, but the rest need to be eaten.

Minerals

Minerals These are the inorganic elements you find in the body, like calcium and iron. Minerals play an important role in keeping the body systems working, and help to build bones and teeth.

Protein rescue

Proteins are the maintenance workers of the body. They help to build and repair your muscles and organs. This makes them a key component of any growing child's diet. Proteins are made from basic building blocks called amino acids. The body breaks down protein in food and turns it into amino acids, it can then change these into different proteins when they are needed.

 Repair The body needs 22 amino acids to keep healthy and maintained.

 Builder Proteins make blood, muscles, and boost your immune system.

17 kJ **Energy** Proteins are rarely used as energy, because of their building work.

 Protect Vitamins A and C help the body protect itself from invaders.

 Builder Skin, cartilage, tendons, organs, and bone all need vitamins.

 Assistant Vitamin B helps the body release energy from chemical stores.

 Repair Minerals help maintain cell chemical reactions and function.

 Builder Bones and teeth get their strength from minerals.

 Balance Water, nerves, and your heart need minerals to work.

The burning energy race...

3 A brisk walk to school every morning can keep you healthy—walking can burn **225 calories an hour!**

4 Jogging can be hard work. In this race it burns the most energy—over **500 calories an hour!** That's a third of what children should eat a day!

Tank full and ready to go—well, nearly. We have fuel and know where it comes from and how to use it. But how can we keep it under control?

Humans love control. Think about watching television. You want to change the channel—what do you do? Scramble for the remote control, of course. It's got to be here somewhere.

This need to control and the built-in desire for it to be convenient happens all over the human body. Your body is doing some amazing stuff without you even being aware of it.

In this chapter, we'll take a look into how your body controls energy. We look at the mastermind behind it all and the control agents it uses to keep a close eye on things.

Control

Brain POWER

The human brain is the most complex organ in the world. It not only houses everything that meaningfully makes you "you"—your conscious thoughts, your personality, your memories—but also processes sensory information, controls your body's movement, and handles millions of other operations at a purely subconscious level. And the best part? It can do all these things at the same time.

ELECTRIC ORGAN

Your brain is made of more than 100 billion neurons, which communicate through electrochemical signals. There are more potential connections between these neurons than there are atoms in the universe.

Most neurons cannot divide and multiply, so take good care of the ones you have!

THINK ABOUT IT

The brain is a pink, jellylike organ that is folded over on itself to maximize its surface area. Each part of the brain specializes in performing certain kinds of tasks.

CEREBRAL CORTEX—this is the wrinkled outer surface of the brain, where most of your thinking goes on.

PARIETAL LOBE—movement, sensation, and spacial awareness.

OCCIPITAL LOBE—processes information from the eyes.

FRONTAL LOBE—conscious thought, personality, and movement.

CEREBELLUM—this fine-tunes muscle movement using feedback from the senses and keeps you balanced.

BRAIN STEM—this is the most basic, core part of the brain. It's responsible for many fundamental, life-preserving functions like breathing and heartbeat, and involuntary actions like blinking. It links the brain to the spine and the rest of the body. Some animals survive with only a brain stem, but they cannot process information in the complex way that higher animals do.

TEMPORAL LOBE—speech, language, and hearing.

Man vs. machine

Writers have been comparing the brain to a computer for decades, but they aren't as similar as you might think. The most powerful computer ever built can run 1.026 quadrillion calculations a second, whereas the human brain can only manage 10 percent of that. But don't be fooled into thinking the human brain is second best. Unlike computers, the human brain is capable of learning and adapting. A computer may be able to beat a human at chess, but it can only perform the functions for which it was designed—a chess computer cannot cook an omelet!

RAPID RESPONSE

The brain isn't just versatile, it's also lightning-fast. Neurons send messages across the brain at around 100 meters per second (225 mph, or 365 km/h). That's nearly as fast as the Bugatti Veyron, the fastest commercial car in the world. But your body can react even faster to situations by bypassing your brain entirely. If you step on a thumbtack, you pick up your foot before you even think about it. This kind of reaction is a reflex triggered by nerves in your spinal cord.

LEFT BRAIN, RIGHT BRAIN

The brain is split into two halves, which are called hemispheres. The left hemisphere controls the right side of the body, and vice versa. They each have different strengths: the left brain plays a crucial role in speech and language, whereas the right brain deals with abstract reasoning.

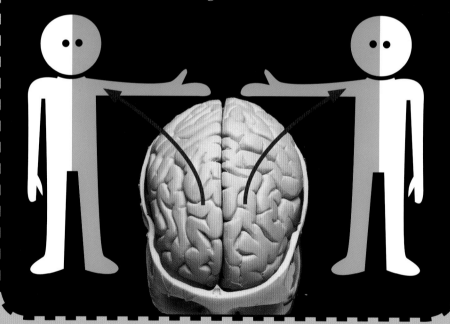

DUAL CONTROLS

There are two types of control systems driving your body. Your conscious brain is constantly making decisions—for example, what to say, or where to walk. Simultaneously, your subconscious is making decisions such as how to keep your balance, or how to keep your body warm.

Here are just a few of the bodily functions your subconscious controls:

Breathing   **Heart rate**   **Hormones**

Blood pressure   **Blinking**   **Digestion**

The brain is only 2% of your body weight but it uses about 20% of the body's energy.

Are you thinking what I'm thinking?

PSYCHOLOGY

The human mind is a rich topic for scientific research. Using modern equipment like MRI scanners, scientists are able to watch different areas of the brain light up as patients think different thoughts. But the mind is still a long way from being fully understood—for example, scientists are still not able to explain the phenomenon of consciousness fully. It's an urban myth that we only use 10 percent of our brains. However, it's certainly true that much of the brain's activity is hidden from our conscious minds. Psychologists like Sigmund Freud have argued that the subconscious is hugely important in shaping our personalities.

Electricity travels directly, like a

GREEK GEEKS — The word ELECTRICITY comes from the ancient Greek word *elektron* (amber), which means "made by the Sun." When you rub amber with a cloth it creates a static electric charge.

DOWN THE WIRE

Electricity is a form of energy. It is carried through a wire by the movement of electrons from one atom to another along a closed loop called a circuit. The source of the electricity, such as a generator or battery, pushes electrons out of its negative terminal. Electrons have a negative charge. The electrons transfer to the next atom in their path, and so on, until they reach the positive terminal at the other end of the circuit.

Insulator

Conductor

STATIC ELECTRICITY

If you rub a balloon along your hair, your hair will stand on end. This happens because of static electricity. As you rub, your hair transfers some of its electrons to the balloon. This leaves your hair with a positive charge. Because like charges repel each other, each hair will try to get as far away from the next one as it can by standing up and moving away from your head.

Moving electrons

Materials with free electrons that can move around allow electricity to pass through them. These materials are called conductors. Materials with electrons that can't move are called insulators. Metals are good conductors, while plastics are good insulators, which is why they are used in electrical cables.

Electric AVENUES
Electricity is all around you. It's in your home, the sky, and **even your body.**

ALL-OR-NONE PRINCIPLE

Nerve cells are a perfect example of the all-or-none principle. When something stimulates a nerve cell, the cell either reacts or it doesn't, like turning on a switch. So, cutting your finger triggers the same impulse as someone stroking your finger. Instead, the strength of the reaction comes from how many impulses are traveling along the nerve per second.

The electrical impulse is passed from one

printer racing the 100 meters.

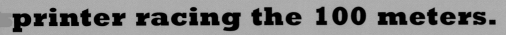

FINISH (A LAMP)

MAGNETISM and electricity are linked. When electrons move through a wire they create a magnetic field around the wire. Similarly, when a magnet is moved along a wire, the magnetic field makes the electrons in the wire move.

Electricity is a form of energy that can travel very quickly and efficiently. **Your body uses electrical impulses to send messages** to the parts it needs to reach. Your nervous system runs on electricity, but it's not the same as the electricity in your home. Your nerves might look like electrical wires, but there's a big difference.

Nerves

A NEURON

Body
Axon terminal
Axon
Dendrite

TYPES OF NERVE CELLS

There are several different types of nerve cells, or neurons, each with a specific purpose.

1. Sensory—these send information picked up by your senses to your central nervous system.

2. Motor—these send information from your central nervous system to your muscles.

3. Interneurons—These link the sensory and motor neurons.

DANGER! Water and electricity
Water and electricity are a dangerous mix. Water conducts electricity very easily. Humans are at great risk of electrocution because our bodies are 60 percent water.

ELECTRICITY IN THE BODY

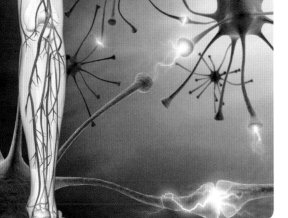

Instead of flowing in a direct line from negative to positive, like electrical circuits, the body uses electricity and chemicals to produce a series of impulses that pass from one neuron to the next. When the neuron body is stimulated, it sends an electrical impulse along its axon to one of its terminals. Each terminal connects to a dendrite on the body of another neuron. Chemicals called neurotransmitters are released to help the impulse move across the tiny gap between neurons. These chemicals make the next neuron fire off a new impulse. This process continues along the chain until the signal reaches its destination.

nerve cell to another, like a relay race.

FINISH (muscle moves)

A TOUCHY subject

Our sense of touch uses the largest organ in the body, the skin. Touch is how we detect physical sensations, such as pressure, temperature, pain, and vibration. Millions of tiny nerve endings are stimulated by the environment around us and send signals about it to the brain. The brain then interprets the signal and tells the body how to respond.

More than just feeling

The ability to feel things is important in keeping us warm, controlling our movements, and avoiding dangerous or harmful substances.

The sensory cortex, shown in red, is the part of the brain that processes signals from the nerve endings in the skin. If you make a slice through it, you can map which section will respond to a stimulus from a particular area of the body.

Cross-section of the sensory cortex

Each area of the sensory cortex connects with the corresponding number on this homunculus.

The sensory homunculus

This monstrous-looking fellow is what humans would look like if our bodies grew in proportion to the amount of brain power needed to interpret all the touch sensory in each body part. As you can see, the most sensitive parts of the body are the hands and lips, while our arms have relatively little in comparison.

This is what we would look like if our bodies

UNDER YOUR SKIN

Our touch sensors are amazing. Not only do they react to pressure, but they also tell the brain whether the stimulus is hot or cold, hard or soft, rough or smooth, wet or dry, and moving or still. Most of our touch sensors are found in the skin. The skin is divided into three layers—the epidermis, or outer layer; the dermis, which contains most of the nerve endings; and the fatty hypodermis, which anchors the skin to the muscles.

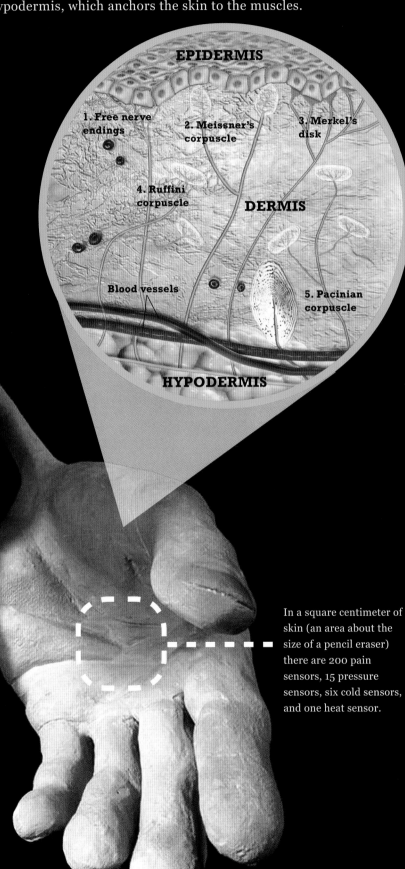

EPIDERMIS

1. Free nerve endings

2. Meissner's corpuscle

3. Merkel's disk

4. Ruffini corpuscle

DERMIS

Blood vessels

5. Pacinian corpuscle

HYPODERMIS

In a square centimeter of skin (an area about the size of a pencil eraser) there are 200 pain sensors, 15 pressure sensors, six cold sensors, and one heat sensor.

HOW DO YOU FEEL?
Well, there isn't just one type of sensory nerve ending—there are FIVE.

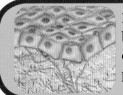

Free nerve endings—these branching nerve endings are found all over the body. They are sensitive to pain, light touch, and temperature.

1

Meissner's corpuscles—found near the surface of the skin, mainly on the fingertips, feet, eyelids, and face. They respond to light pressure and tickling.

2

Merkel's disk—also known as junction nerves, they are found in the upper layers of the skin and sense continuous light pressure and textures.

3

Ruffini corpuscles—these oval-shaped cells are located deeper in the skin. They sense when the skin is stretched, and help you grip things.

4

Pacinian corpuscle—these are found deep in the skin near joints and muscles. They sense more sustained pressure and vibrations, such as when you exercise.

5

Internal sensors—Nerve endings also play a role inside the body. When your bladder is full, it stretches the nerve endings in the surrounding tissue, creating discomfort and an urgent need to run to the bathroom!

were in proportion to our touch sensors.

Secretion AGENTS

The brain is the control HQ of the body, and the nervous system is its speedy messenger service. But it can't run everything alone; it needs help from special secretion agents called HORMONES.

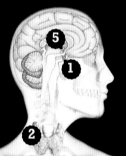

Hormones are chemicals made by the body that help control certain body systems, like metabolism, growth, and sexual reproduction. Hormones are water soluble and dissolve into the blood. Their special skill is that they target specific cells, effectively carrying out their mission objectives.

Hormones are made in the brain and other organs known as glands. They are part of the endocrine system and secrete their hormones directly into the blood.

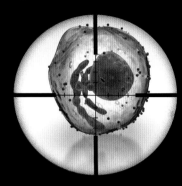

1 PITUITARY GLAND
This pea-sized gland is located in the brain and makes the growth hormone that controls your physical development.

2 THYROID GLAND
The thyroid gland is found in the neck and its hormones help with breathing, circulation, and energy conversion.

3 PANCREAS
The pancreas resides above the stomach and makes insulin, which helps the body use sugar (glucose) as its main energy.

4 OVARIES (women)/ TESTES (men)
The sex glands produce the sex hormones, estrogen (women) and testosterone (men). These help control puberty and fertility.

5 HYPOTHALAMUS
Controls the secretion of other glands and links the nervous system to the endocrine (hormone) system.

6 ADRENAL GLANDS
These sit on top of the kidneys and produce epinephrine (adrenaline), which acts to stimulate and protect the body from danger.

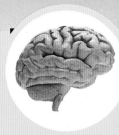

BRAIN—More oxygen and fuel (glucose) is transported to the brain. Now your brain is energized and ready for anything.

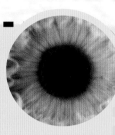

EYES—Epinephrine enlarges the pupils in your eyes. This allows more light in, and more light means more information and awareness of surroundings.

MOUTH—Epinephrine makes the smaller blood vessels in your mouth constrict. This reduces the blood supply and makes your mouth feel dry.

SWEAT—Smell the fear. Epinephrine triggers your apocrine sweat glands. This type of sweat contains fatty oils, which react with bacteria, making you smell.

What makes us jump out of airplanes?

We must have a screw loose! Actually, we are fueled by the thrill hormone—epinephrine. Here's a lowdown on what happens to your body when it kicks in.

PAIN—An adrenaline rush is normally followed by an increase in endorphins (chemicals released by the brain that make you feel good). Endorphins also suppress pain— handy in moments of danger!

DIGESTION—In a state of emergency, digestion isn't at the top of your body's to-do list. Epinephrine suppresses nonvital systems, allowing oxygen and fuel to get to the places that need it.

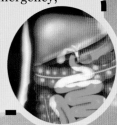

MUSCLES—More oxygen and fuel (glucose) means more energy to help you move. Your muscles are ready to lift, fight, run, duck, dodge, or throw—basically anything!

HEART—Your stroke volume (how much blood is pumped) and heart rate increase. This helps to supply your body with more oxygen and fuel, as well as remove waste products.

BREATHING—Breathing can become more rapid to increase oxygen levels in the blood, as well as getting rid of built-up waste gases. Epinephrine also helps to expand your airways, so you breathe in more air with each breath.

FIGHT or FLIGHT

When the body is in danger or under stress, its survival instincts kick in. This is known as the fight-or-flight mechanism and epinephrine plays a major role. Epinephrine is released into the blood and is pumped around the body. Its main mission is to protect and ready the body for physical action, be it fighting back or running away.

TOP SECRET

What makes a hormone? Most hormones are proteins. Their long molecules are made from carbon, hydrogen, oxygen, and nitrogen. Some hormones also contain some of the body's trace elements, like sulfur and iodine.

Gamma rays X-rays Ultraviolet light

Visible light

Wavelength

ENERGY WAVES

Light is a form of energy. Like most energy, it travels in waves. Wavelength is the distance between wave peaks or troughs. It tells us how much energy waves carry. The shorter the wavelength, the higher the energy. Different wave types can be ordered on a spectrum, from dangerous high-energy gamma rays to safe low-energy radio waves. Visible light is only a small section of this spectrum.

SEEING WAVES

Natural light from the Sun looks white, but if you take a closer look it is actually a rainbow of colors. In 1665, Sir Isaac Newton discovered how to split light, using prisms and lenses. Each color of light travels at a different wavelength. The human eye can see from violet to red. But light energy doesn't end there—the other wavelengths are just invisible to the human eye.

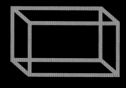

WHY DO HUMANS HAVE TWO EYES?

Our eyes are set apart and see slightly different images. The different views are then overlapped in the brain to create a 3-D image and help us judge distances.

SEEING IS BELIEVING

The eye allows us to see by intercepting light waves and turning them into electrical impulses for the brain to interpret. Everything you see is actually a mental reconstruction of the light that has bounced off an object.

Energy

Would you be surprised to hear or read that your senses are all about energy? Seeing and hearing are two important senses we use all the time. They are also perfect examples of how our bodies make use of the different energy forms around us.

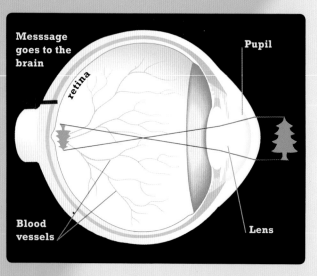

Messsage goes to the brain

retina

Pupil

Blood vessels

Lens

EYES SEE...

The eyeball is a spherical sac of fluid with an opening at one end and a nerve at the other. As light waves enter the eye, the lens focuses them onto the retina at the back of the eye. This turns the image upside down, but the brain flips it the right way up. There are two types of light-sensing cells in the retina, called *cones* and *rods*. Cone cells are sensitive to color and detail. There are far fewer rod cells, which are sensitive to low light conditions. Colors and detail are therefore easier to see in well-lit areas.

B
O D
Y S C
I E N C E
C A N Y O U
R E A D T H I S

Infrared light	Microwaves	Radio waves

SEEING THINGS

Light travels in straight lines. When light waves hit an object they bounce off. It is these bouncing waves that travel into the eye. When no light source is present, there are no light waves, so we don't see anything.

SOUND ENERGY

The sound energy we hear is different to the energy waves above. Audible sounds are transmitted by air molecules vibrating. When something vibrates, the air molecules around it are pushed together, leaving an empty gap behind them. With each vibration, groups of molecules are pulsed toward the ear, where they are collected for processing.

SENSES

Radio waves are at the slow end of the energy wave range. We can't hear them directly, since our bodies are unable to trap and interpret them. Instead, we use a radio receiver, which converts the radio wave energy into sound waves.

TINY BONES

The inner ear has the smallest bone in the human body—the stirrup. It is only 0.1 inch (2.5 mm) long!

GOOD VIBRATIONS

The ear collects and turns sound waves into recognizable noises. For this delicate job the body uses three tiny bones—the *hammer*, *anvil*, and *stirrup*. Vibrating air molecules channeled into the ear hit the eardrum. This makes the inner ear bones vibrate and transfers the energy into the fluid-filled tubes of the cochlea. The vibrations travel through the fluid, disturbing tiny hairlike cells, which convert the vibrations into signals that the brain can interpret.

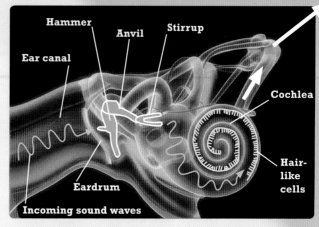

Messsage goes to the brain

Hammer
Anvil
Stirrup
Ear canal
Cochlea
Hair-like cells
Eardrum
Incoming sound waves

PERFECT VISION

The idea of 20/20 vision comes from being able to read an eye chart 20 ft (6 m) away. You can have better eyesight: 20/10 means you can read at 20 ft (6 m) what most people can read at 10 ft (3 m). A hawk, if it could read, would have 20/2 vision!

SMELL MOLECULES

What are smells? Actually, they are molecules that float around in the air, called *odorants*. We breathe in these molecules and our nose uses chemistry to detect the smell. An average person can recognize about 4,000 different smells, and someone with a well-trained nose can sniff out nearly 10,000! Smell is also linked to taste, and about 70 percent of what we think of as being a taste is actually detected by our nose.

Where seeing and hearing are about physics, **taste and smell are all about chemistry**. Smell and taste are linked—not only are the two systems

Gone to your head
Both your smell and taste senses are connected by nerves directly to the brain.

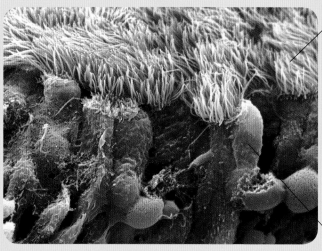

Cilia

The cells that line the nasal cavity are topped by tiny hairlike structures called cilia. The cilia sweep the mucus toward the back of the nasal cavity and down into the throat, taking dirt and other particles with it.

Cell

A NOSE FOR CHEMISTRY
Your nose is a finely tuned smelling machine. As air is drawn into the nostrils, it is warmed, and any dirt and dust is trapped by hairs and mucus. It then passes into the nasal cavity, which is covered in even more mucus. The odorants dissolve in the mucus and are detected by sensory cells. Each cell detects a specific type of chemical. These send signals to the brain, which figures out what the smell is.

Try holding your nose while you eat something. What happens to the taste? Why would a blocked

Smelly dog
Dogs can be 10,000 times more sensitive to odors than humans. Yet a human smell sensor cell is just as sensitive as a dog's. So, what makes dogs such expert sniffers? Although their sensors are the same, they have many more of them (1 billion in dogs compared with only 10 million in humans).

SENSES

physically close to each other in the head, but they both also interact to tell us as much as possible about the substances we eat and breathe into our bodies.

It's all
in the mind!

TASTE MOLECULES

Tasting works in a very similar manner
to the way you smell things. The key to taste lies on your tongue and in your saliva. Taste is linked to smell and sight, and both senses help trigger saliva production. Real mouth-watering stuff! As you eat, the chemicals that make up food dissolve into the saliva and are identified by the thousands of taste buds on your tongue. There are five main tastes: bitter, sour, salt, sweet, and umami, a savory flavor. Taste buds can detect all five, but are better with some tastes than others.

Most of your taste buds sit on your tongue, but you also have some on the roof of your mouth and in your throat.

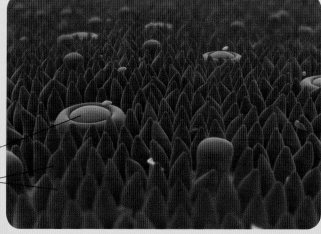

Taste bud

Papillae

TONGUE ACTION
The surface of the tongue is covered by lots of tiny bumps, known as papillae. Between these bumps sit the taste buds. The taste buds are made up of lots of sensory cells, like segments in a orange. Tiny hairs on the top of these cells extend upward and it is here where the dissolved molecules lock on. The cells send signals to your brain, which adds in signals from the nose and tells you what the substance tastes like.

Why do we need smell and taste?
There is a very good reason why we need to be able to taste and smell things—so we don't poison ourselves. Nasty tastes and smells are usually associated with toxic gases, decaying food, or poisonous plants, all of which could

Acquired tastes
Our taste buds are more sensitive when we are younger, which explains why some children react strongly to some flavors that adults enjoy. As you get older, your taste buds lose their sensitivity and you even start liking vegetables!

How many SENSES?

You can count the number of body senses on one hand? Wrong.

SENSING THE WORLD

Why are senses so sensible? Senses are important because they let us understand the physical and chemical world around us. This awareness of the environment is vital to our survival, from gathering food, avoiding danger, to finding other people. We communicate using our senses—we talk, listen, gesture, and touch. The extra senses follow the same mantra as our core five—they help us understand our surroundings. Here's a lowdown on these extra senses and how they help us survive the everyday as well as the extreme.

STRETCH Deep in your muscles are special receptors that allow your brain to know which muscle is moving and how hard it is working. Without these receptors the body wouldn't know what it was doing. So, even standing still would be tricky, let alone trekking through the cold Arctic wilderness.

6

Some people believe they have a sixth sense. Well, they do—we all do. We also have a seventh, eighth, ninth, and tenth sense. Our extra senses are all related to our main five, and are just as important when it comes to sensing the world around us.

 GRAVITY Living on Earth means dealing with gravity. Small receptors in your inner ear called otoliths let you know which way is up and which is down.

MOTION Movement would be impossible without the motion sensors in your inner ear. If you spin around you can confuse your motion senses, making you dizzy.

 **HEAT** Heat receptors sense external temperatures, from icy weather to hot drinks. They are all over your body, with your lips and tongue being most sensitive. These senses even work at a distance.

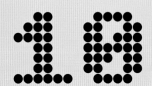 **PAIN** There are pain receptors all over your body. Wouldn't life be more painless without pain receptors? Yes, but they do fulfill a very important job. They help limit damage and injury. When the body senses pain, it tells you not to use that area. So a bad leg makes you limp, protecting the injury—vital on long icy adventures.

ANIMAL SENSE

The ten human body senses help our bodies to work, but they are aren't the only senses in the natural world. Some animals use other senses to help them survive.

SHARK
In the nose of these marine predators are hundreds of electrosensors. Sharks use them to detect electrical signals let off by prey in distress.

BAT
Finding dinner in the dark isn't an easy job, unless you are a bat. They possess a kind of radar, called echolocation. This helps them lock onto flying insects.

BEE
Bees don't have a map to help them find their way—or do they? Bees have a ring of iron oxide inside their bodies and scientists believe it could act like a compass.

EARTHWORM
It doesn't look very tasty, but the earthworm is tastier than you think—its whole body is covered in chemoreceptors. So, it's like one big tongue.

MIXING Senses
We know that taste and smell are closely linked. But can your senses truly mix? Our senses are converted into signals for the brain to interpret. It is here where senses can overlap. People can develop a condition known as *synesthesia*, meaning their senses mix. This can make certain tasks seem easier. For example, some successful musicians hear musical notes as different colors, so when they write songs it's more like painting a picture.

A handy tool

Have you ever needed a helping hand? Well, you have an amazing tool on the end of each arm. Our hands have played a handy role in our survival as a species, as well as dealing with modern life. What is so amazing about the hand? It's all about control and movement. The hand can be precise and delicate—it can run thread throught the eye of a needle. But it can also be strong and powerful—it can crush, grip, and punch. This variety of action is down to four key handy components—bones, nerves, muscles, and tendons. The hand has 27 bones, 4 main nerves, and is controlled by 40 muscles and 40

tendons. Your hand also holds some fantastic attachments that make it a gripping machine. On your palm and fingertips are lots of tiny grooves that increase the force of friction and improve your grip. Also, on the end of each finger is a hard nail that allows you to pinch and pick very small items, like knots. On top of this is the mighty thumb. Our thumbs give us the upper hand. They are opposable, which means you can touch your little finger with your thumb. Without this special skill you would struggle to grip and hold. Try this at home—tape your thumb to your hand and try tying your shoelaces with just your fingers.

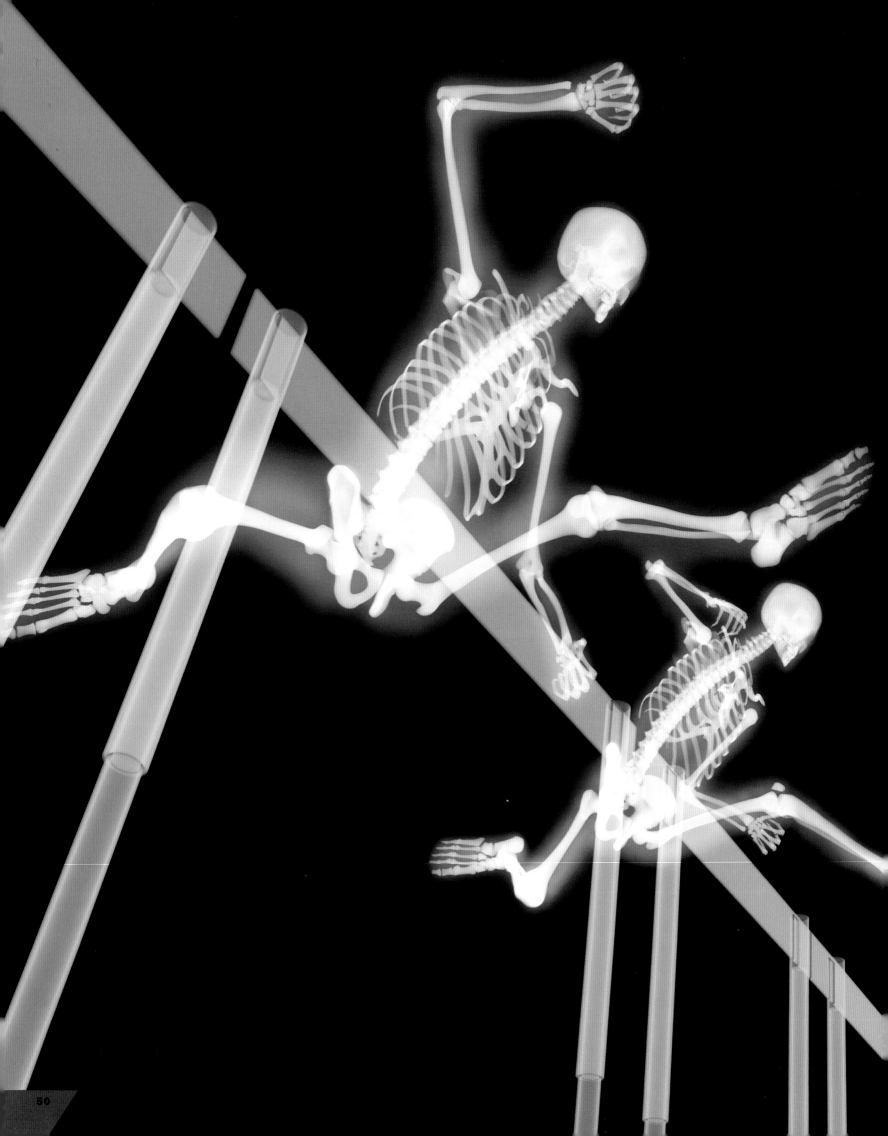

Done. You've got energy covered and know how to control it. The next big hurdle is movement. It seems simple enough, since you move around every day. True, but there's more to moving than just walking or standing.

Movement is all about laws; not the police, but laws discovered by a guy named Sir Isaac Newton. Forces make us move and stop. But where do these forces come from and what's the science behind them?

Movement isn't just limited to walking. Inside your body millions of little movements are happening every second. And how does where you are affect how you move?

In this chapter, we're going to be moving through the different types of forces, their impact on the body, and how the body reacts to them. So, let's get moving…

Movement

NEWTON'S laws

Movement is all about forces. Whether you are moving steadily, speeding up, or even just standing around, there are forces at work. In 1687, English scientist and mathematician Sir Isaac Newton figured out three laws that explain why and how things move.

Sir Isaac Newton (1643–1727) was responsible for many great scientific discoveries in optics, mechanics, and mathematics. While pondering why the Moon stayed in orbit around the Earth, he reputedly saw an apple fall from a tree. He realized that the same force, which he called gravity, was pulling both it and the Moon toward Earth. More usefully, it was helping him keep his wig on.

Law one

"An object that isn't **PUSHED** or *pulled* by a force either stays still or keeps moving in a straight line at a constant speed."

Law two

"Forces make things *accelerate*. The **BIGGER** the force, and the lighter the object, the greater the *acceleration*."

Law three

"Every **ACTION** has an equal and *opposite reaction*."

1

A force is simply a PUSH or a PULL. To make an object move, you need to apply a force. You will need another force to stop it.

It is easy to see how something standing still needs a force to get it moving, but why does it keep going? The perfect example for this law can be seen in space. Because there is so little matter in outer space, there is nothing to offer any resistance. If an astronaut pushes off, he will continue in a straight line, at the same speed, until another force stops him or speeds him up.

2

We can use this law to explain throwing a baseball a given distance. If you are trying to get a runner out, you need to get the ball to the base before he does. A baseball is light, but you have to throw it hard to make it accelerate faster than the runner. However, you would need even more force to make a bowling ball reach the base first.

To a scientist, acceleration means speeding up, slowing down, or changing direction.

An athlete running experiences the forces of friction, gravity, and air resistance acting against his forward movement.

3

This law is a little more complicated and looks at forces working in pairs. When you run, the force of your foot pushing on the ground sends your body forward. This also produces an opposite reaction, the ground moves away with an equal force. You are, in fact, making Earth turn under you by the teeniest amount. The thing to remember is that although the forces might be equal, their effects might not be.

When you push off from the block, the block pushes back at you equally hard.

Body FRICTION

Take a close look at your skin, and you'll see that it's covered in tiny grooves. Even at a microscopic level, its surface is rough and bumpy. Which is just as well, because it's the rough texture of your skin that creates friction, which enables you to pick things up. Friction may be most famous as the force that slows things down, but it's also essential to many of the functions our bodies perform.

Good Friction

Somebody help me— I can't stop!

GRIPPING—Without friction between your body and the world, you wouldn't be able to grip on to anything. Performing the simplest tasks would be like juggling wet soap. Getting from one place to another would also be a problem, since moving around would be like running on ice.

EATING—Your teeth use friction to tear food apart and to crush it up. Without friction you wouldn't be able to chew well at all.

Muscle fibers are like long cables.

MOVEMENT—Your muscles are made up of tiny fibers. When the muscle contracts, these fibers slide against each other and shorten. Friction between these fibers keeps the movement under control.

SENSES—Your sense of touch relies on friction. If your skin were perfectly smooth, things would slide quickly off it, leaving your nerves with little to sense.

Under a microscope, skin looks anything but smooth.

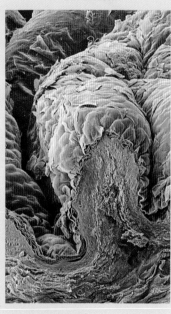

Harnessing friction

Friction can be a useful ally on the sports field. Take soccer cleats, for example. The cleats increase the friction between the playing surface and your feet, so you can get more grip for running, dribbling, and shooting!

Have you ever tried to start a fire by rubbing two sticks together? The friction between the sticks causes heat, which ignites the fuel. Matches also use friction to create a flame.

When a match head is scraped along a rough surface, the friction mixes flammable chemicals together.

Sliding friction

There are several different types of friction. Sliding friction slows down objects that are already moving. This is the kind of friction between moving skis and snow, or between your bike's tires and its brakes.

Static friction

Static friction is the resistance that has to be overcome before an object can START moving. It's much stronger than sliding friction. Imagine pushing a desk across the floor: it takes much more of a push to start it moving than it does to keep it going.

Real friction

Oh, my poor aching joints!

DRAG—As we move through air or water, we come up against a kind of friction called drag. It pushes back against our movements, which means we have to work harder to get anywhere.

JOINTS—Normally bones are protected from the constant wear and tear of friction by a protective, cushioning layer (see below). A disease called osteoarthritis can destroy this layer between bones. This can make joints swell up and become painful.

BLISTERS—Blisters are one of the most common sports injuries. Blisters appear at friction hot spots—for example, where your sports shoe rubs against the back of your heel, or where an oar rubs against your palm. The friction makes layers of the skin separate from each other. Either the epidermis (the outer layer of skin) separates from the dermis, or the epidermis itself comes apart.

FRICTION BURNS—Friction produces heat, and friction between your skin and a rough surface can easily give you minor burns. If you've ever tripped and skidded across a rough surface like Astroturf, you'll know exactly what a friction burn feels like.

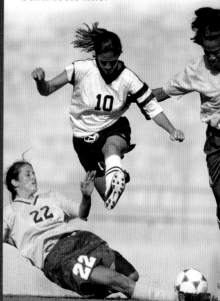

Fighting friction

To move smoothly, your body needs to overcome the friction between the parts that make it up. Your joints are protected by smooth cartilage, which covers the ends of bones and stops them from grinding against each other. Joints are also filled with a liquid called *synovial fluid*, which acts like the lubricating oil in a machine. Without these friction fighters, our bones would quickly get worn down.

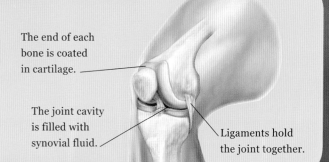

The end of each bone is coated in cartilage.

The joint cavity is filled with synovial fluid.

Ligaments hold the joint together.

Muscle POWER

Muscles are the powerhouses of the body. They use the chemical energy you have eaten and stored as ATP and turn it into kinetic energy. Muscles generate the force and power to move your body. They pump your blood, draw oxygen into your lungs, and keep you standing up—nearly everything you do needs muscle power.

Muscle types

There are three main types of muscles in your body. Each has a different role.

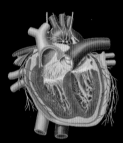

CARDIAC—This type of muscle is found only in the heart. The muscles act as a single unit and are involuntary, meaning they work without you having to think about it.

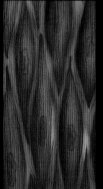

SMOOTH—Made up of long, thin cells, this type of muscle gets its name from its smooth appearance. Smooth muscle is also involuntary and is found in your internal organs, such as the arteries, stomach, and bowel.

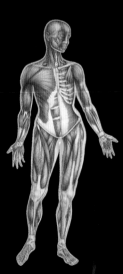

SKELETAL—These muscles are attached to your skeleton and help you move. These are voluntary muscles, so you tell them when to work. They are sometimes called striated muscle, because of their "striped" appearance under a microscope.

THE POWER OF MUSCLES

Skeletal muscles can produce an incredible amount of force. This strength comes from the shortening, or contraction, of the fibers that make up the muscle. When you think about moving, the brain sends a signal to the relevant muscle telling it to contract. The amount of force produced by the muscle depends on how much the brain tells it to contract.

Feel the force

Muscles are attached to the bones by strong pieces of fibrous tissue called tendons. Tendons are slightly elastic. They stretch across a joint to the next bone. When a muscle contracts, the tendons pull the bone toward the muscle. Tendons provide the muscle with extra leverage and increase the amount of force the muscle can supply.

Muscles that make joints straighten are called extensors.

When a muscle is relaxed, its fibers spread out.

Tendon

Muscle

Muscles that allow joints to bend are called flexors.

Tendons

Full stretch
There are limits to how much a muscle can move. Special sensors in the muscles detect stress and tension, and ensure that the muscle does not stretch or contract too far or too fast. If this happens the muscles and tendons could tear.

When a muscle is contracted its fibers are close together.

INSIDE A MUSCLE

Muscles are bundles of fibers.

Myosin and actin microfilaments.

Inside each fiber are thinner fibers called myofibrils.

Each set of fibers is wrapped in a membrane.

Muscles are made of hundreds of tiny fibers. Inside these fibers are even thinner fibers, so the whole structure is like an electrical cable. At the very core are two microfilaments (really tiny fibers) called myosin and actin, which slide over and grip each other tightly. It is these actions that make muscles contract.

The heart is the hardest-working muscle in the body.

FAST AND SLOW

The fibers that make up muscles can be divided into two main groups, fast-twitch and slow-twitch muscles. Each muscle has a mixture of the two fiber types. In a healthy human there is usually a 50–50 split between fast- and slow-twitch fibers.

Catch me if you can!

FAST TWITCH

Fast-twitch muscles contract quickly and generate high levels of power. However, this means they tire very quickly and are better for short, sharp bursts of activity.

I think I'll stick to walking...

SLOW TWITCH

These are smaller than fast twitch and generate less power because they contract about 20 percent slower. However, they don't tire as easily and are good for low-level activities, like walking and long-distance running.

TEAMWORK

Forces work in opposite pairs and so do muscles. Everything about muscles is teamwork, from their tiny fibers locking together, to how they make joints move. But muscles can only pull, they cannot push.

SKELETAL MUSCLES

All the skeletal muscles work in pairs. When one muscle contracts, the partner muscle relaxes and lengthens. The contracting muscle is called the *prime mover*, while its relaxing partner is known as the *antagonist*. These roles can switch, depending on the movement of the joint.

I get a real kick out of doing this.

Antagonist

Prime mover

When you are about to kick a ball, the muscle at the back of your thigh (the prime mover) contracts to pull the lower leg backward.

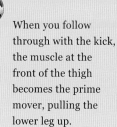

Antagonist

Prime mover

When you follow through with the kick, the muscle at the front of the thigh becomes the prime mover, pulling the lower leg up.

Lifting weights can make muscles grow, which is why bodybuilders have bigger muscles than ordinary people.

There are more than 30 muscles in your face, which allows you to make different expressions.

You use your quadriceps muscles for running, jumping, and cycling.

The biggest muscles are in your bottom.

Made of muscle

There are more than 600 muscles in the human body. Muscles are what give your body its shape and provide 25 to 45 percent of its mass. Exercise helps keep the muscles in peak form. Some of the most powerful muscles are in the back, attached to the spine. These help you stand upright. They also provide the power to lift and push things. A number of muscles often act together to provide a complete range of movement, such as twisting or rotating.

It will beat about 2.5 billion times in a lifetime.

MOVE your body

So far, we've looked at body movement in terms of generating energy, controlling it, and converting it into muscle power. But there are also **two types of movement—linear and angular**. Linear movement is getting from A to B, while angular movement is what your body does to make this happen. When it comes to movement, your joints play a vital role. There are several different types...

perform a variety of different movements, from jumping and running, to balancing and standing still.

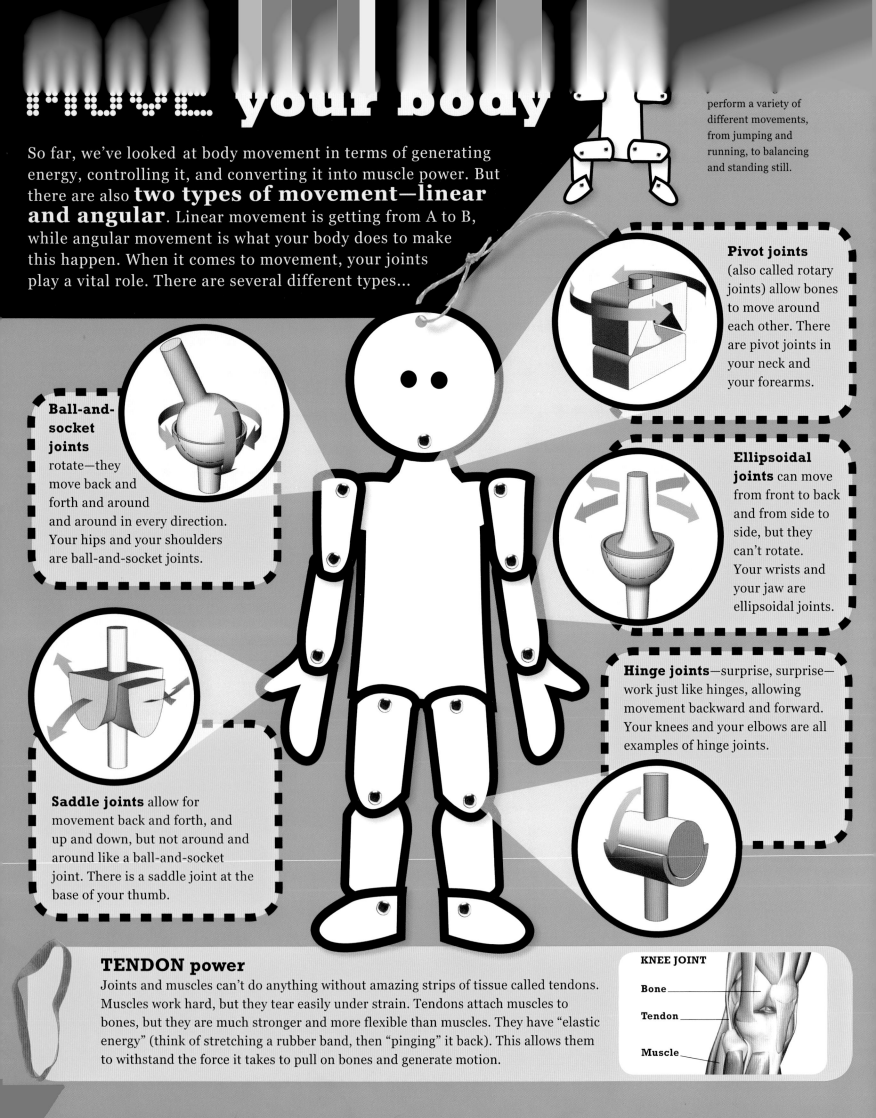

Pivot joints (also called rotary joints) allow bones to move around each other. There are pivot joints in your neck and your forearms.

Ball-and-socket joints rotate—they move back and forth and around and around in every direction. Your hips and your shoulders are ball-and-socket joints.

Ellipsoidal joints can move from front to back and from side to side, but they can't rotate. Your wrists and your jaw are ellipsoidal joints.

Hinge joints—surprise, surprise—work just like hinges, allowing movement backward and forward. Your knees and your elbows are all examples of hinge joints.

Saddle joints allow for movement back and forth, and up and down, but not around and around like a ball-and-socket joint. There is a saddle joint at the base of your thumb.

TENDON power

Joints and muscles can't do anything without amazing strips of tissue called tendons. Muscles work hard, but they tear easily under strain. Tendons attach muscles to bones, but they are much stronger and more flexible than muscles. They have "elastic energy" (think of stretching a rubber band, then "pinging" it back). This allows them to withstand the force it takes to pull on bones and generate motion.

KNEE JOINT

Bone

Tendon

Muscle

MOTION

LINEAR MOTION is exactly as it sounds—movement forward or backward in a straight line. We can measure linear motion using certain variables: distance, displacement, speed, velocity, and acceleration.

Displacement and distance on face value sound very similar. But displacement is the shortest route in a straight line between start and finish, whereas distance measures the distance actually traveled.

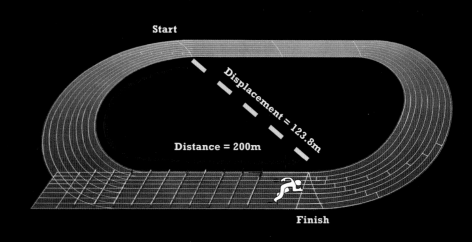

Start

Displacement = 123.8m

Distance = 200m

Finish

Speed and velocity also get mixed up. Speed is easy to figure out since you simply divide the distance by the time it takes to get there. Velocity is how fast you move in a particular direction. So, if you run at 12 mph (20 km/h), but in a circle, your speed will remain the same, but your velocity will be different because you are constantly changing direction.

Distance ÷ time = SPEED

Acceleration can be confusing. To accelerate doesn't just mean speeding up—it also means changing direction, or even slowing down! (But if we slow down we say acceleration is negative.)

The golfer swings at the ball—and the club *accelerates*.

Animal	SPEED mph	ACCELERATION ft/s²
Human		
Lion	50	31
Gazelle		
Cheetah	65	33½
Elephant		

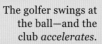

Speed and acceleration

Here is some speed and acceleration data for humans—and some pretty fast animals, too! Speeds are measured in miles or kilometers per hour, and acceleration in feet or meters per second squared. So what you learn from this chart is that a human can only accelerate at around 11½ ft/s² (3.5 m/s²), whereas a lion and cheetah can pick up speed much more quickly. Not only that, but they also run much faster than you. Better to stay away!

EARTH forces

Gravity is one of the most important forces in the universe. It is also very important on Earth because it keeps us from floating away into space. As a force, gravity has affected how our bodies work. Our systems have adapted to its persistent force over the millennia of evolution. The circulation system, for example, uses muscles and valves in our veins so that blood can flow up as well as down. **Gravity also affects how we move**.

First, let's look at gravity and how it pulls on the body. Gravity is alway present—pulling you to Earth. Usually, the ground is in the way and you don't really notice it. So, the best way to show its effect is to take a dive off a high dive.

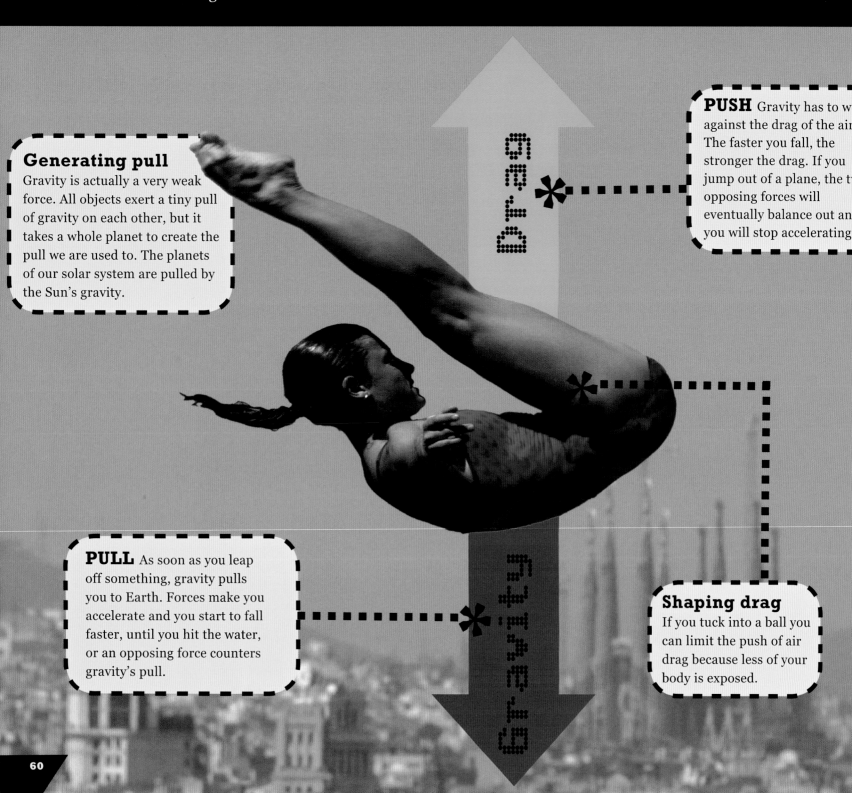

Generating pull
Gravity is actually a very weak force. All objects exert a tiny pull of gravity on each other, but it takes a whole planet to create the pull we are used to. The planets of our solar system are pulled by the Sun's gravity.

PUSH Gravity has to w against the drag of the air The faster you fall, the stronger the drag. If you jump out of a plane, the t opposing forces will eventually balance out an you will stop accelerating

PULL As soon as you leap off something, gravity pulls you to Earth. Forces make you accelerate and you start to fall faster, until you hit the water, or an opposing force counters gravity's pull.

Shaping drag
If you tuck into a ball you can limit the push of air drag because less of your body is exposed.

COG in motion

We know that gravity pulls and the air resists. But how does gravity hinder us when we try to move? The matter that makes our bodies is pulled down by gravity and it is this that gives us weight. Movement is all about how the body balances its weight so we don't fall over. This balancing act is affected by your body's center of gravity (COG). This is the central concentration of your body's weight. To make sure you don't fall over you must keep your COG inside your supporting base. So, if you stand still, your base is the length of your feet. Lean too far forward and you'll topple over.

Standing still

The art of standing still is to make sure your COG stays between the limits of your stable base. You can improve your stable base by standing with your feet farther apart. But watch out, your COG can move left to right as well as forward and back, and having one foot too far in front of the other may make you fall sideways.

base

COG

When the COG leaves your base, you'll fall over.

base

Running

All the motion in running, especially when changing direction, can alter your COG. Our skill of balancing while moving comes from our ability to bend and adapt. If we were rigid, like a car, and the COG moved outside our base, we would topple over. Being able to bend and counterbalance gives us a greater sense of balance and stability. Also, the COG, and therefore our weight, is slightly forward, helping us to move. Try this at home—run in a wide arc to your left; which way does your body bend?

base

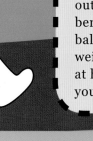 **=Center Of Gravity**

Ski jumper

Equipment can help stabilize the body. A ski jumper leans forward to accelerate down the slope. The long skis give him a long, stable base, so he can lean farther than if he were wearing normal shoes. As he lands, he keeps his feet slightly apart under his shoulders, giving him a long and wide stable base.

base

ARCHIMEDES' Principle

On his discovery Archimedes jumped out and ran down the street shouting EUREKA! (I have found it!)

What's scientific about bathtime?

As the great Greek mathematician Archimedes stepped into his bathtub, he noticed the water level rose. Archimedes discovered it is not only the weight of the object that affects if it floats or sinks, but also how much water it displaces. With this "eureka" moment, Archimedes had discovered the force of buoyancy.

WET forces at play

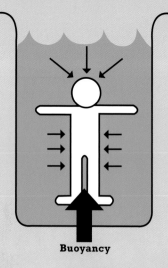

Buoyancy
When an object is submerged the surrounding water exerts a force on the object from all directions. The overall effect is an upward force.

Gravity
The mass of any object is affected by the downward pull of gravity. (Mass measures how much matter something contains.) The force produced by gravity acting on an object's mass is called weight.

WATER Forces

Water is denser than air and traveling through it is much harder. Also, gravity isn't the only force in play; there's another you have to deal with—buoyancy. To float or not to float isn't your choice. Instead, it comes down to a simple principle discovered over 2,000 years ago.

Floater or sinker
The interaction between the two forces of buoyancy and gravity decides if an object floats or sinks.

If the force of buoyancy is greater than the force of gravity, the object will float.

However, if the force of gravity is greater than the force of buoyancy, the object will sink. The heavier something is, the more likely it is to sink.

Not all heavy things sink. An oil tanker floats because it displaces lots of water and its weight is less than the weight of the displaced water. So, weight and volume are very important. If the oil tanker kept its weight, but was the size of a canoe, it would sink without a trace because it would be heavier than the volume of water displaced.

WATER resistance

Much like traveling through air, there is a similar resistance force at play in water. Water resistance can be a drag, so to move through water means generating enough force to overcome it. Try walking through knee-high water—not as easy as walking down the street!

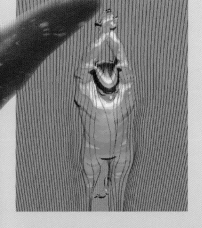

The red areas show the parts of the body that experience the highest resistance as the swimmer travels through water. Dark blue shows areas of least resistance.

SHARK TECHNOLOGY

The shark is a master predator of the deep and can reach speeds of 68 mph (110 km/h). Swimwear manufacturers have examined sharkskin to find out how this speedy fish beats water resistance.

Tiny ridges in the shark's skin channel water, reducing resistance.

The fabric of the sharkskin inspired swimsuit copies the ridge effect.

SWIM LIKE A SHARK The new technology of the sharkskin inspired swimsuit reduces the water resistance by about 4 percent. It doesn't sound like much, but when Olympic swimmers dive into the pool, it could make the difference between a gold or silver medal.

Brace for IMPACT

Football players are big-framed, heavy guys, but they're not lumbering hulks—they can pound down the field at up to 20 mph (32 km/h). They know that the faster they move, the harder they hit, which is why they drive their bodies forward into tackles like muscular battering rams. When they collide, the impact force is determined by multiplying mass by acceleration. So that combination of weight and speed can result in some real bone-crushing, eye-watering power.

The AVERAGE LINEMAN charges his victim

1 newton = The force necessary to accelerate a mass of

160 kg (350 lb) ACCELERATING at 6 m/s²

=

F = ma

(the BIGGER and

force = mass x acceleration

1 **2** **3** **4**

The more momentum a player has, the harder he is to stop. When a defender tackles or blocks, he's trying to change his opponent's momentum, by applying a force in the opposite direction. Enough force will make them both grind to a halt.

as much force as having a **BABY ELEPHANT** dropped on you!

faster you are, the harder you hit)

Taking the STRAIN

The streets are no longer just for pedestrians, cars, and pigeons. A new mover-and-shaker has claimed rights to the block. **Free running** is a modern version of *parkour*, which started in urban France during the 1990s. It is a form of street gymnastics, in which participants use walls, stairs, benches, and balconies as apparatus to perform jumps, somersaults, and balances in a continuous, flowing style.

Strains and sprains happen when you are not fully warmed up or make movements that overstretch the muscles.

Repeated exertion can damage the body's shock absorbers and lead to arthritis and other problems.

The body's ability to generate, handle, and counter force is amazing. One modern sport that takes the body to its limits is **free running**. With all the running, jumping, and somersaults involved, the body takes a pounding. Just landing after a running jump exerts a force of ten times your body weight. But **where does this force and its energy go?**

SHOCK, RATTLE, AND ROLL

The force created by landing on concrete can be truly shocking. However, the body can take the pressure using its own built-in, high-performance shock absorbers—the knees. The amount of force they have to cope with depends on whether the knees are bent, the softness and slope of the landing surface, and the forward motion of the jumper. Jumping exerts 900 pounds (400 kg) of force on each knee joint.

cross-section

Shock absorbers in cars are pumps filled with gas that absorb energy from a spring and transfer it to a piston. The piston pushes against the gas, which slows it down and turns the energy into heat.

BONES AND MUSCLES

The knee is the largest joint in the human body. It has four bones, of which the thigh bone (femur) is the biggest bone in the body. Bones are very good at resisting crushing and absorb some of the impact energy. The muscles attached to the bones also help absorb energy. The thigh bone has two large muscle groups, the quadriceps and the hamstrings, on the front and back of the leg.

Femur

LIGAMENTS

For the bones to work at their best, they need to be stable. This is where ligaments come into play. These tough bands of tissue are made of dense fibers and hold the bones together. Ligaments are surprisingly tough—twice as strong as nylon rope—and keep the joint in place no matter what the movement or impact.

Tibia

Simply bending your knees for climbing creates a force of 300 pounds (135 kg) on your knee joints.

CARTILAGE

When bone hits bone it can really grate, especially when friction is involved. This is where cartilage comes in. This tough, smooth tissue covers the ends of the bones, allowing them to slide over each other, and stops them from wearing away. It is also used to join tendons and ligaments to bones. Cartilage can endure up to 7 tons of force before it snaps, perfect for protecting the bones. It is also flexible and cushions most of any impact.

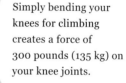

Synovial fluid

CAPSULE

The knee joint is known as a synovial joint. A capsule of thick, stringy fluid surrounds the joint, offering further protection. The fluid nourishes the joint, keeping it fit and healthy, ready for the next impact. Wearing correctly designed footwear can reduce the impact of landing by up to 20 percent—so if you are planning to go street running it's better for your knees if you wear cushioned sneakers instead of your school shoes!

Ligament

Under Pressure

The human body is an adaptive machine. Change the environment, and the forces and pressures that act on the body change, making it harder to **survive** but not impossible. Here's a look at the highs and lows of **extreme forces.**

OUTER SPACE

Beyond the Earth's atmosphere is outer space. Space is a weightless environment, and there is little gravity. Removing this important everyday force means your body's everyday systems, bones, and muscles work differently. You can't move your arms and legs as you would do on Earth, so they lose density and weaken. So, when you return to Earth, you get light-headed and need a helping hand as you come out of the shuttle.

Floating around space in a hi-tech, modern spacesuit looks like fun, especially compared to the extreme harshness of space. But it isn't as cozy as it looks. Living inside a spacesuit is actually like being at the top of a very high mountain, and living up there isn't easy...

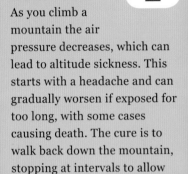

SICK OF ALTITUDE

As you climb a mountain the air pressure decreases, which can lead to altitude sickness. This starts with a headache and can gradually worsen if exposed for too long, with some cases causing death. The cure is to walk back down the mountain, stopping at intervals to allow the body to get used to normal air pressure.

The highest mountain on Earth is Mount Everest. Its summit towers 29,028 ft (8,848 m) above sea level. No one lives there but many have climbed its treacherous slopes. In this extreme environment the forces the body deals with every day at sea level change dramatically. It all has to do with pressure, or more precisely, air pressure.

SEA DEEP

Deep below the waves there is a truly alien environment. Little light penetrates the deep, and, with all the weight of the water above pressing down on you, you begin to feel its effects. High pressure causes matter, especially gas, to compress, making it compact into a denser form. As you come back up, the gases in your body begin to expand again. So, divers swimming back to the surface have to swim slowly and stop at intervals. Swim too quickly and the diver would suffer from decompression sickness (the bends), which can be fatal.

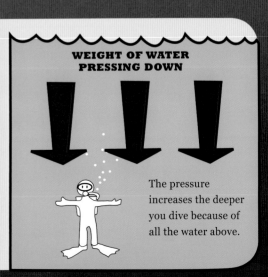

WEIGHT OF WATER PRESSING DOWN

The pressure increases the deeper you dive because of all the water above.

GRAVITY

NO GRAVITY

Blood forced down

Blood pumped up

ON EARTH

IN SPACE

UPSIDE-DOWN SYSTEMS
In space our body systems don't work as they do on Earth. Let's look at how blood travels around the body. On Earth our bodies have to work against gravity, especially when pumping blood to the brain. In space there is no gravity to work against, but our circulation system doesn't know this and too much blood is sent to the brain and less goes to the legs. This gives astronauts big puffy heads and skinny legs.

The human body can survive in space without a suit, though only for 15 seconds. The dangers are the low pressure, extreme temperatures, and radiation. Also, don't hold your breath—it will make your lungs explode!

When you leave the safety of sea level, pressure on the body changes. But how does the body react?

MOUNTAIN HIGH

As you climb up a mountain people say the air is getting "thinner." Actually there is the same concentration of oxygen at the top of Mount Everest as there is at sea level. The difference is AIR PRESSURE. In our lungs, oxygen moves into our blood because of the pressure difference between our blood and the air outside. The greater the difference in pressure, the easier oxygen diffuses. On top of a mountain the pressure difference isn't as high as it is at sea level, so with each mountaintop breath less oxygen enters our blood. With less oxygen to fuel your body, simple activities prove to be a challenge— even standing up can be tricky.

LOWER PRESSURE

OXYGEN
21%

NITROGEN
78%

The concentration of gases in the atmosphere remains the same.

SEA LEVEL

Our bodies are made mainly of water, which means even at extreme depths the water pressure will never crush us. However, solids and gases are affected and it is dangerous to dive deeper than 330 ft (100 m), although with special breathing equipment I could dive to 1,050 ft (320 m).

AROUND THE BENDS
What are the bends? Having dived deep underwater, the high pressure compresses gases in the body. As the diver swims back to the surface these compressed gases, mainly nitrogen, expand as the pressure reduces. This causes bubbles to form in the blood, tissues, and organs. Depending on the location of the bubbles, the symptoms can be anything from headaches and dizziness, to extreme limb pain and lung failure. If left untreated it can be deadly.

Physical UPGRADE

Do you want to be stronger, faster, or more flexible? Think of your body as a blank canvas that can be customized to your own design. It's fine-tuned to the kind of activity you put it through—whether that's deep-sea diving, weightlifting, or channel surfing.

No pain, no gain

When a body builder has a tough workout, he's making tiny tears in his muscle fiber—which is every bit as painful as it sounds. Those microtears make muscles feel sore a day or two after exercise. You'll know the feeling if you've ever been on a long run.

As a result of damage to the muscle tissue, chemical signals are sent through the body. These instructions tell your muscles to create new tissue as they recover.

Body builders must strike the right balance between putting stress on muscles, and letting them recuperate. Recovery time is crucial, since this is when the new muscle tissue actually forms.

Ultimate lungs Free divers can boost their lung capacity to 10 liters or more—they can breathe in a third more air than most people. They build up their lungs using a technique called packing, where they breathe in then breathe in again, compressing all the air into their lungs.

Bending over backward Olympic gymnasts need to be incredibly flexible as well as strong. They use exercises like splits, high kicks, and backbends to stretch their tendons and muscles, and to increase their range of motion.

This strongman has built up his muscles enough to move a 8.6 ton truck single-handedly.

How far could YOU move a truck that size?

Wouldn't it be faster if he got in the cab and started driving?

Use it or lose it
Astronauts barely have to use their muscles at all to move around in low gravity, but they exercise for more than two hours a day. If they didn't, their muscles would gradually waste away.

What's the point of exercise?
Regular exercise isn't just about shedding fat. It can transform your whole body.

 Joint mobility It helps you twist and flex without effort.

 Muscle strength It makes you lean and mean.

Bone density It helps build strong bones.

 Heart strength It keeps you healthy and energetic.

 Immune system It helps you fight off infection.

 Brain function It helps you concentrate better and respond faster.

 Coordination It makes your brain and body work better together.

Body at **WAR**

Your body is constantly under siege from tiny but ferocious alien invaders, called germs or pathogens. But your body is protected by a whole host of defensive measures, including strong outer walls, chemical alarm systems, and stalwart defenders in the form of white blood cells like macrophages.

Your body's surface is crawling with millions of germs, but these marauders need to get inside to cause infection. The dead outer layer of your skin acts as a solid barrier to keep them out.

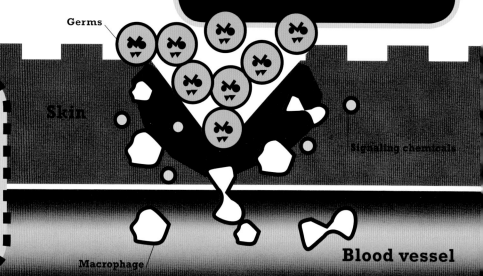

Germs

Skin

Signaling chemicals

Macrophage

Blood vessel

1

When germs enter your body through a cut, specialized skin cells release signaling chemicals to summon macrophages to the area. Macrophages engulf some germs and carry them away.

Macrophage

2

The germs rapidly multiply inside your body. Meanwhile, the macrophages carry germs to B cells. These are factories for making antibodies—biological weapons designed to attack that specific germ.

B cell

Antibodies

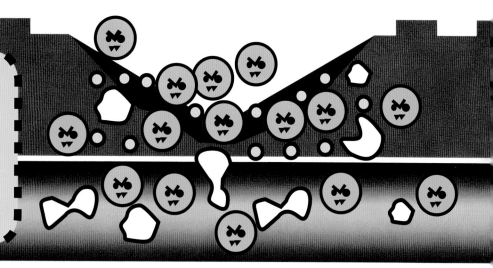

3

Antibodies travel through the blood to the infected area and fix on to the germs. They send out signals to macrophages and other germ-engulfing cells called phagocytes, which digest the germs.

Phagocyte

Antibody

Phagocyte

Body invaders

Germs leach our bodies' nutrients, and may also produce toxins. There are three main families of germs: bacteria, viruses, and protists.

Bacteria are single-cell organisms that can be helpful or harmful to people.

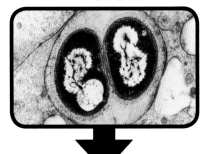

Viruses are tiny particles that take over cells and use them to reproduce themselves.

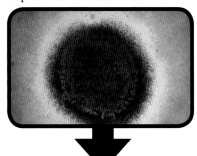

Protists are moisture-loving single-cell organisms. They cause diseases like malaria.

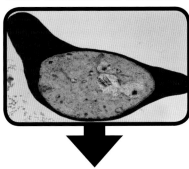

Body defenders

All white blood cells are produced in the bone marrow. When germs attack, your body responds by flooding the infected area with white-blood-cell-rich blood. That's why your skin turns red and swells up.

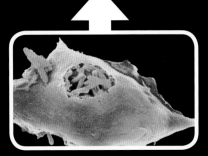

Macrophages are a kind of phagocyte that engulf germs and that carry them to B and T cells.

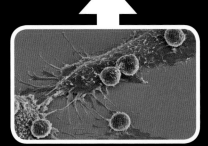

B & T cells (also called B and T lymphocytes) make antibodies and give orders to other white blood cells.

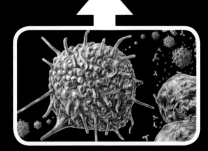

Antibodies have specialized projections that can fasten on to one particular kind of germ and disable it.

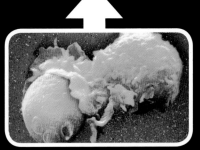

Phagocytes are white blood cells that fold their outer membranes around germs, then digest them.

INNER ARMOR

The lymphatic system is your body's infection-fighting rapid-response system. This network of channels runs through your entire body and connects together immune command centers called lymph nodes. These nodes produce B cells and T cells, which coordinate your body's response to infection. White blood cells can easily move between blood vessels and lymph vessels.

The thymus, spleen, and parts of the lower intestine are connected to the lymphatic system, and each plays an important role in your immune response.

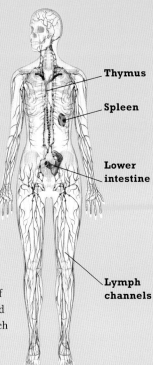

Thymus

Spleen

Lower intestine

Lymph channels

Extra protection Your body uses several other mechanisms to protect you from infection. You can add a further barrier by washing your hands.

Strong acid in your stomach kills the germs in your food.

Saliva, tears, sweat, and urine wash germs out of your body.

Mucus traps germs, and coughing or sneezing propels them away.

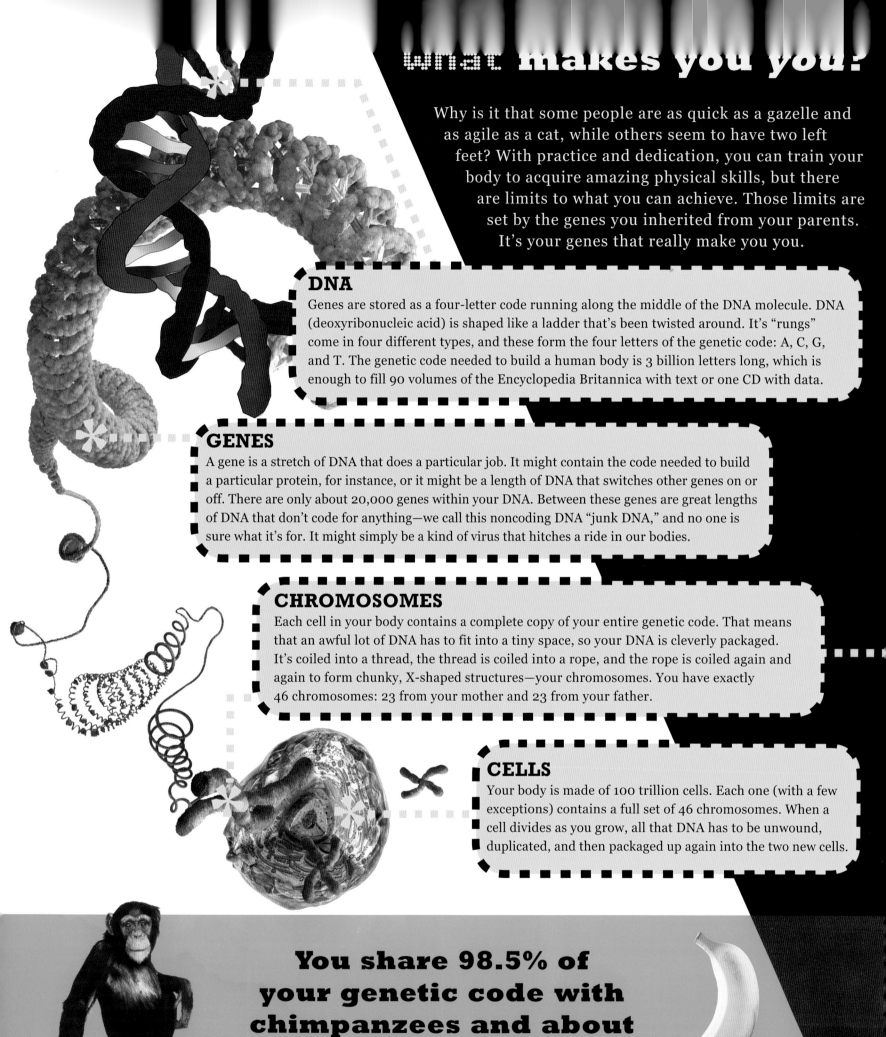

What makes you you?

Why is it that some people are as quick as a gazelle and as agile as a cat, while others seem to have two left feet? With practice and dedication, you can train your body to acquire amazing physical skills, but there are limits to what you can achieve. Those limits are set by the genes you inherited from your parents. It's your genes that really make you you.

DNA

Genes are stored as a four-letter code running along the middle of the DNA molecule. DNA (deoxyribonucleic acid) is shaped like a ladder that's been twisted around. It's "rungs" come in four different types, and these form the four letters of the genetic code: A, C, G, and T. The genetic code needed to build a human body is 3 billion letters long, which is enough to fill 90 volumes of the Encyclopedia Britannica with text or one CD with data.

GENES

A gene is a stretch of DNA that does a particular job. It might contain the code needed to build a particular protein, for instance, or it might be a length of DNA that switches other genes on or off. There are only about 20,000 genes within your DNA. Between these genes are great lengths of DNA that don't code for anything—we call this noncoding DNA "junk DNA," and no one is sure what it's for. It might simply be a kind of virus that hitches a ride in our bodies.

CHROMOSOMES

Each cell in your body contains a complete copy of your entire genetic code. That means that an awful lot of DNA has to fit into a tiny space, so your DNA is cleverly packaged. It's coiled into a thread, the thread is coiled into a rope, and the rope is coiled again and again to form chunky, X-shaped structures—your chromosomes. You have exactly 46 chromosomes: 23 from your mother and 23 from your father.

CELLS

Your body is made of 100 trillion cells. Each one (with a few exceptions) contains a full set of 46 chromosomes. When a cell divides as you grow, all that DNA has to be unwound, duplicated, and then packaged up again into the two new cells.

You share 98.5% of your genetic code with chimpanzees and about 50% with bananas!

Blame your parents

Do you have curly hair? Freckles? Skinny legs? Blame your parents—all your physical characteristics are set by the genes they gave you. You've actually got two whole sets of genes: one set is on the 23 chromosomes you inherited from your mother, and the second set is on the 23 chromosomes from your father. If there's anything you don't like about your body, it's your parents' fault. Or your grandparents'.

Among the 46 chromosomes that everyone has are two special ones: the sex chromosomes. These are shaped like the letters X and Y. Your mother has two X-chromosomes, but your father has one X and one Y.

I've got the X-FACTOR!

BOY OR GIRL?

Your gender is set by your two sex chromosomes. You get one of these from your mother and one from your father. Your mother can only pass on X-chromosomes, but your father can pass on either an X or a Y. If you get an X from your father, you're a girl. If you get a Y, you're a boy. It's the luck of the draw.

Nature vs. Nurture

Your genes set many of your characteristics, from the color of your eyes to your height. But they don't have absolute control. You can change your body by how you eat and exercise. You can also program yourself to learn new skills like swimming or skiing. Genes have a major influence on mental characteristics such as intelligence and personality, but scientists are undecided as to whether genes (nature) or experience (nurture) has the greatest effect.

You're UNIQUE

The chromosomes you inherited from your parents aren't simply copies of theirs. Each of yours contains reshuffled bits and pieces from your grandparents' chromosomes, giving you a totally unique combination of genes (unless you have an identical twin). You can see your uniqueness in things like your fingerprints and iris pattern.

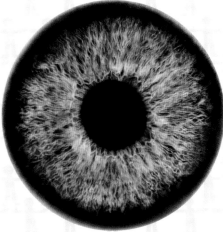

The iris is a ring of colored muscle fibers around the pupil.

I see it in your eyes

The colored parts of your eyes—your irises—are as unique as fingerprints, thanks to their distinctive pattern of stripes and gaps. An iris scanner can read this pattern like a barcode and confirm your identify. But criminals can fool the system with printed contact lenses.

Biting an apple isn't a crime. Biting a person is.

Bite prints

Your teeth and the bite marks they leave are unique to you. Forensic scientists sometimes use "bite prints" to identify criminals, but the technique is not 100% reliable.

Fingerprints

Police have been using fingerprints to catch criminals for more than a century. Recently, fingerprint scanners have become a feature of laptop computers. With some ingenuity, these scanners can be fooled by fake prints glued on to your fingers.

Fantastic. You can energize yourself, control it, and move on up in life. The world is your oyster. So, what's left in life? Well, there's one horizon still out of reach—the future.

Science has given us so much, we know how to build a body, how to control forces, and how we became who we are. So what does the science of the future promise?

Modern science is progressing quickly. The microchip, nanotechnology, and genetics are opening doors and even windows to new possibilities.

In the following pages, we're going to have a peek into the future and see what science is working on today and what it predicts for tomorrow. From rebuilding the body, to choosing genes, and unearthing mysteries. So, let's enter the time machine...

Future

Dead body SCIENCE

When a dead body is found and the cause of death looks suspicious, the police call in forensic scientists to search for every tiny clue. Forensic scientists can tell a lot from a dead body, no matter how rotten and decayed it is. And if the cause of death is murder, the evidence scientists collect can track down the killer.

Count the clues...

The crime scene

The first stage of investigation is to seal off the crime scene so that the evidence can't be disturbed. The body is photographed before being removed, and its outline is drawn on the ground in chalk. The positions of the limbs may reveal whether the victim fell violently, was dumped, or lay down before dying. Forensic scientists comb the entire crime scene for the tiniest clues: hairs, spots of blood, fibers from clothes, fingerprints, footprints, and any dropped objects, from bullet casings to shards of glass. Every speck of evidence is bagged, labeled, and taken back to the lab.

POSTMORTEM

After a suspicious death, a specially trained doctor called a pathologist performs a kind of operation called a postmortem. The naked body is examined for injuries or signs of a struggle (such as damaged fingernails). Next it is cut open and each organ is inspected for signs of damage or disease that might reveal the cause of death. If the body has decomposed, an insect expert identifies the maggots and beetles that have infested the flesh. These can reveal how long the body was left to decay.

Clue 2

Clue 4

Footprints that don't match the victim's shoes may have been left by the killer. In addition to revealing what kind of shoes the killer wears, the prints are clues to the killer's sex, height, and weight.

A dropped wallet is sure to contain fingerprints. If items are missing, the killer may have been a thief or may have faked robbery to hide their true motive for murder.

POLICE LINE

of blood splatters can reveal the path of a bullet or the type of injury a victim suffered.

FACIAL RECONSTRUCTION

When a person dies, their body decomposes (rots). Soft, fleshy parts such as the eyes, skin, and muscles rot and disappear quickly, but bones and teeth last much longer. When bones and teeth are all that remain, a forensic scientist can still tell a lot about the person's age, sex, build, and ethnic background. A forensic artist can even re-create the shape and appearance of a person's face by using a model of the skull to rebuild facial muscles. This technique, called facial reconstruction, has helped police solve murders committed decades ago. It has even been applied to ancient Egyptian mummies to reveal what the Egyptians looked like thousands of years ago.

FINGERPRINTS

Look carefully at your fingertips. The skin is covered with swirling grooves that improve your grip just as the tread of a boot or a tire improves grip. Along the tiny ridges of skin are microscopic glands that secrete grease and sweat for even better grip. When you touch anything, your fingers leave an almost invisible print made of grease from these glands. Forensic scientists can reveal the prints with a sprinkling of dust and then record them with adhesive tape or a photograph. If the prints match those of a suspect, then the police have proof that the suspect was present at the crime scene.

Clue 1

Fingerprints can identify who the criminal is. No two people on Earth have the same fingerprints—not even identical twins.

DNA FINGERPRINTING

Just as everyone's fingerprints are unique to them, so is everyone's DNA—the molecule that carries genes. After a murder, investigators search both the crime scene and the victim's body for traces of the criminal's body fluids in order to obtain a sample of DNA. DNA can even be extracted from hairs. To make the DNA "fingerprint," forensic scientists break down the DNA into chemical fragments and then make these spread out through a sheet of jelly to form a pattern of stripes that's unique to every person (except for identical twins). The chance of an accidental match with a suspect's DNA is less than one in a million.

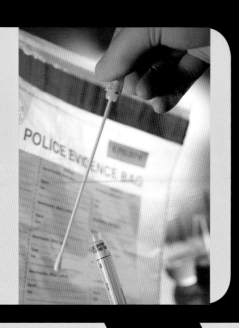

Thanks to DNA fingerprinting I'm more than just a brilliant detective—I'm a gene-ius!

DO NOT CROSS

REENGINEERING the body

When a car needs to be repaired after a crash or a breakdown, ordering spare parts is easy. Not so for the human body. You only have one heart, one liver, one stomach, or just a pair of many other organs. If disease or injury damages your organs beyond repair, your life could be cut short. In years to come,

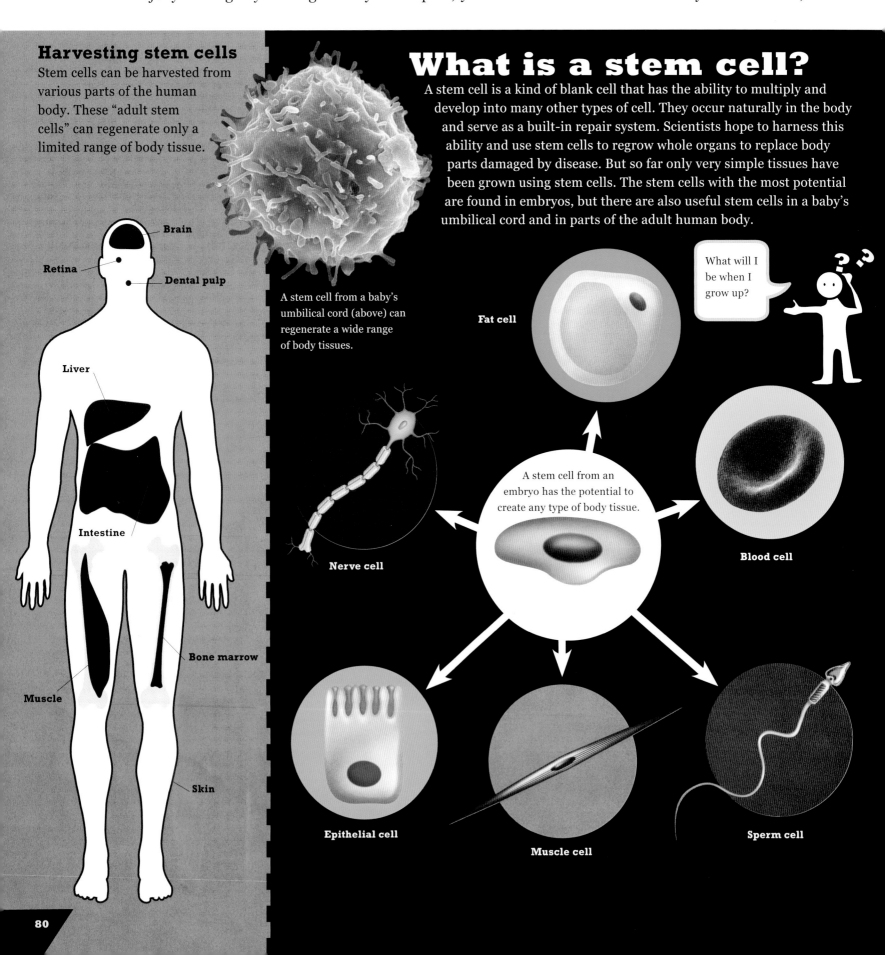

Harvesting stem cells

Stem cells can be harvested from various parts of the human body. These "adult stem cells" can regenerate only a limited range of body tissue.

Brain

Retina

Dental pulp

Liver

Intestine

Muscle

Bone marrow

Skin

A stem cell from a baby's umbilical cord (above) can regenerate a wide range of body tissues.

What is a stem cell?

A stem cell is a kind of blank cell that has the ability to multiply and develop into many other types of cell. They occur naturally in the body and serve as a built-in repair system. Scientists hope to harness this ability and use stem cells to regrow whole organs to replace body parts damaged by disease. But so far only very simple tissues have been grown using stem cells. The stem cells with the most potential are found in embryos, but there are also useful stem cells in a baby's umbilical cord and in parts of the adult human body.

Fat cell

What will I be when I grow up?

A stem cell from an embryo has the potential to create any type of body tissue.

Nerve cell

Blood cell

Epithelial cell

Muscle cell

Sperm cell

however, scientists might find a way of regrowing spare parts of your body. **Research** into stem cells, cloning, and genetic engineering could lead to an **amazing range of new treatments** that can keep your body in tiptop shape throughout your life. But such research is presenting some **difficult questions**.

Genetically engineered humans are still science fiction, but genetically engineered crops are a reality.

Genetics was pioneered by an Austrian monk, Gregor Mendel in the 1850s. Although today, the science of genetic engineering arouses resistance from many religious corners.

Skin graft
Even without using stem cells, scientists can regrow some parts of the body. Thin sheets of skin can be grown from live skin cells and then grafted over wounds such as burns to repair them.

Designer babies
Some people think that genetic technology will one day allow us to choose the genes our children get, enabling us to create custom-made "designer babies" who grow up to be highly intelligent, good-looking, and so on. But this technology may never be truly possible, since many of our genes interact in complex ways.

PRO
Scientists conduct research into genetics and stem cells not to enhance the human body but to fight disease. Such research could lead to the discovery of life-saving drugs and new ways to replace damaged organs.

CON
However, many people say it's wrong to experiment with embryos that have the potential to become individual human beings. Some people also think it's wrong to "play God" and interfere with nature by altering genes.

Cloning

Dolly the sheep was created by cloning. She was the world's most famous sheep.

Cloning is nothing new. Identical twins are natural clones that form when an embryo splits in two, and many plants and animals can produce offspring by cloning themselves. In recent years, scientists have figured out how to make artificial clones by taking the nucleus out of a normal body cell, inserting it into an egg cell, and then zapping it with electricity to activate it so it can develop into an embryo. Cloning can already by used to create genetically identical copies of animals. The real benefit, however, might come in the future when scientists have figured out how to use embryonic stem cells to regrow whole organs. When this becomes possible, doctors will be able to take any cell from your body, turn it into a cloned embryo, and then use the embryonic stem cells to regrow your organs and cure you of disease.

We have the same DNA.

Surgery SCIENCE

We're lucky to be living through a medical revolution.

Modern science is constantly finding new ways to repair and transform bodies: failing organs can be replaced and shattered bones can be repaired. Surgeons can remodel faces and bodies to make people look more normal, or to help them stand out from the crowd—or even to turn them into a work of art.

Keyhole surgery
A very small cut is made in the patient's body, through which a camera and tiny instruments are inserted. The surgeon watches on a screen as he performs the operation.

BODY MECHANICS
Surgeons are the service engineers of the human body. They use tools to cut into and physically repair or reshape the bodies of patients. Surgery is at the cutting edge of modern science. It is already common for robots to help perform complex operations in the least invasive way. In the near future, it may be possible to clone replacement organs from a patient's own cells.

It can be a little tricky, but brain surgery is hardly rocket science!

Anesthesia
There are two kinds of anesthetics. Local anesthetics make one part of your body feel numb, whereas general anesthetics make you lose consciousness completely.

Sterilization
Surgical staff must protect patients from infection. Before starting an operation they "scrub up" by washing thoroughly and putting on disinfected gowns and masks. Surgical instruments are cleaned with ultrasound, heat, and disinfectant chemicals.

Brain fixers
During brain surgery, a piece of the skull is removed to give surgeons access to the body's most complex organ. Some brain operations are performed with only local anesthetic, so that surgeons can see how the patient's reactions are affected.

Organ transplants
If an organ starts to fail, a replacement can be transplanted from a living or very recently deceased donor. The organ is packed in ice during transportation, and the recipient is given drugs to stop her immune system from attacking the new organ.

Surgical timeline

Earliest known form of surgery is trepanation (drilling holes in the skull).

Napoleonic wars—first modern surgery performed by barber surgeons.

James Blundell performs first successful blood transfusion.

Modern anesthetics like chloroform begin to be used in surgery.

Plastic fantastic

Plastic surgery can make a dramatic difference to the lives of people who have been horribly disfigured by injuries or disease. Isabelle Dinoire lost her lips, chin, and most of her nose when she was mauled by her own labrador. She could barely speak or eat. But in November 2005 she was given the world's first partial face transplant.

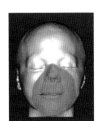
Scar tissue was removed before the transplant.

Blood vessels were connected to the new face.

Five months later, Isabelle could feel with her new mouth.

 vs.

Plastic extreme

Some people have taken the idea of body transformation to its outer limits. As far as they're concerned, the more people stare in the street, the better. Native American Stalking Cat has had a series of operations on his body to turn him into his totem animal, the tiger.

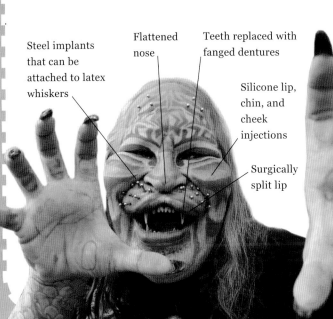

Steel implants that can be attached to latex whiskers

Flattened nose

Teeth replaced with fanged dentures

Silicone lip, chin, and cheek injections

Surgically split lip

BODY BEAUTIFUL?

Many people have something they dislike about their bodies, and today an increasing number of people are opting to have these "imperfections" reworked under the knife of a cosmetic surgeon.

Face lift (rhytidectomy)

By tightening the skin on the forehead, surgeons can make wrinkles disappear. They cut a line along the hairline, detach the skin from the face, then pull everything up before letting it heal.

I want to look like Brad Pitt...

Eyelid surgery (blepharoplasty)

Eyelid reshaping is the most common form of cosmetic plastic surgery in East Asia. Half of people there don't have a double-crease in their eyelid, and some feel it's more attractive to have one.

Nose reshaping (rhinoplasty)

Large noses can make people very self-conscious. Surgeons can change the shape of a nose by making small incisions inside the nostrils, then remodeling the bone and cartilage.

Fat removal (liposuction)

In this operation, a small hole is made in the skin of the abdomen through which a narrow tube is inserted. This tube is moved around to break up fat, which is then sucked up the tube.

The body REBUILT

When the human body fails, technology can rebuild it.

BLADE RUNNER

Oscar Pistorius is an athlete who blurs the boundary between disability and superability. A double amputee since he was eleven months old, Oscar has been nicknamed "Blade Runner" after his amazing prosthetic legs. These legs, the *Ossur Cheetah Flex-Feet*, are used by many Paralympic competitors. But Oscar has gone a step further, by beginning to compete in able-bodied track and field meets. This has created a debate among fellow competitors. The *Flex-Feet* give Oscar the ability to run stride-for-stride with able-bodied sprinters, but do they also give him an unfair advantage? Are they better running machines than normal, flesh-and-blood legs? Let's take a closer look at this technology.

As the *Flex-Foot* hits the track, its J-shaped curve acts like a spring, compressing and storing potential energy. When the athlete moves forward, the curve returns to its original shape and releases its stored energy as a forward push.

Prosthetic timeline

Golden artificial eye (found in Shahr-i Sokhta, Iran)

Artificial toe (found on Egyptian mummy)

Bronze artificial leg (discovered in Capua, Italy)

First dentures

First artificial heart implant

The human body is a complex and powerful machine. But for all its wonder it is also fragile and can easily be damaged beyond biological repair. Using pioneering science and technology, we're increasingly finding ways to rebuild the body, swapping muscles for motors, and nerve fibers for microchips.

There's no simple answer to the question of whether *Flex-Feet* offer an advantage over conventional limbs. On the plus side, the prosthetic allows the the athlete to run using about 25 percent less energy. However, the spring effect of the *Flex-Feet*, which return 90 percent of the energy put into them, is much weaker than the push of real feet.

The *Flex-Foot* is made from carbon fiber. This lightweight material has superior strength, durability, and flexibility.

The *Flex-Foot* also acts as a shock absorber, reducing impact on the knee, hip, and lower back. This means that athletes can train for longer.

Heart of steel In extreme circumstances, it's possible for the human heart to be removed and replaced with a mechanical pump, which uses hydraulic force to push blood around the body. During the seven-hour operation, the patient is kept alive by an external heart–lung machine. The artificial heart is powered by internal and external batteries.

The AbioCor is the world's first completely self-contained replacement heart. It is only implanted if all other options, including normal heart transplants, have been exhausted.

Eye spy Ocular prosthetics are often called glass eyes, though most are actually made of acrylic. While they may look like a real eye, they don't provide sight. However, they do help to smooth social interactions, in which eye contact can play an important part.

Custom-made ocular prosthetics have hand-painted pupils, which are a perfect match for the patient's working eye.

Bionic arm Former US marine Claudia Mitchell lost her arm in a motocycle accident. Now she's become the world's first real-life bionic woman, after an operation that connected nerve endings in her chest to an artificial arm. She can operate the three motors in the mechanical arm with her thoughts. The arm also sends signals to the brain through her nerve endings, which allow her to feel with it.

 First face transplant operation

 First mind-controlled bionic arm

⊙ First bionic eye operation

2005   2006   2008

Future SENSES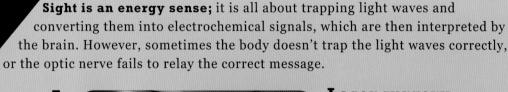

Plug my new senses in!

Senses help us see, feel, hear, taste, and smell the world around us.
But, sometimes our senses go a little haywire, perhaps breaking down completely or deteriorating with age. Don't worry, we are resourceful beings and have long helped our failing sight and hearing with external devices like glasses and hearing aids. But these can be crude and old fashioned; surely science has more to offer? Let's see what's in store for our future senses.

FIXING Sight

Sight is an energy sense; it is all about trapping light waves and converting them into electrochemical signals, which are then interpreted by the brain. However, sometimes the body doesn't trap the light waves correctly, or the optic nerve fails to relay the correct message.

Glasses act as an external lens to help bend the energy waves onto the correct area of the retina, allowing you to see clearly. There are two common ailments that require glasses—nearsightedness and farsightedness. You are nearsighted when your lens is too curved and it focuses the light waves in front of the retina. Farsighted is the opposite: the lens is too flat and focuses the light waves beyond the retina. Both form a blurred image.

Contact lenses offer an alternative to glasses, providing a more subtle sight fix. However, because they sit on the eye there is a limit to how thick or curved they can be, so in extreme cases glasses are the only option.

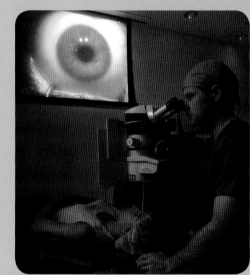

Laser surgery
Recent scientific advances have given us laser refractive surgery. The procedure uses a laser to reshape the lens so it correctly focuses the incoming light waves onto the retina. The procedure isn't permanent and several treatments might be necessary. Also, the operation takes place while the patients are awake! But don't worry, they are given local anesthetic.

FUTURE Sight

As we learn more about the brain we can start to help our senses. How? Well, it all comes down to interpreting external energy waves. If we can plug adaptations into our brain we can even cure blindness.

Video glasses
The future of glasses is already here. The Dobelle Artificial Eye is a video camera mounted on a pair of glasses and connected to electrodes implanted into the brain. The device allows patients to see outlines of shapes, large letters, and numbers on contrasting color backgrounds.

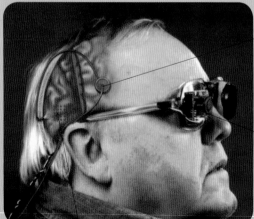

Input to brain

Video camera

Electrodes

Optic nerve

Retina

Microchip implant

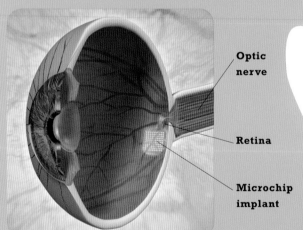

Chip and see
If you don't want to walk around with a pair of bulky video glasses, then the retina implant might be for you. Still being developed, it acts in the same way as the light-sensitive cells in the retina, reading the incoming light waves and sending signals to the brain via the optic nerve.

Pardon?

Sight makes sense now, but what about sound? Hearing is also an energy sense, which makes it easier to combat any ailments. Injury, illness, and old age can all affect your body's ability to read and transfer sound vibrations. Don't worry, we've heard there are some solutions.

The air-conducting hearing aid sits on top of the ear and feeds a small, thin plastic tube into the ear. The hearing aid captures and amplifies sound vibrations. It has been around for a while and works in a similar way to the old-fashioned ear trumpet, by focusing sounds onto the eardrum.

In-ear hearing aids offer a more discreet and less bulky alternative. They work along the same principles, of translating and amplifying sound waves. They can also be finely tuned to the wearer's individual needs, as some people struggle with certain sound frequenices.

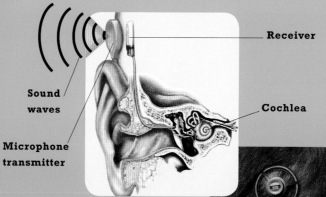

Receiver

Sound waves

Cochlea

Microphone transmitter

Bionic ear

The bionic ear is actually a cochlear implant. It works differently than a regular hearing aid. Instead of amplifying sound waves it transmits to and stimulates functioning sound cells and nerves in the cochlea. An external microphone sends electrical impulses straight to the cochlea. It can help deaf people to hear sounds and clearly pick out speech in quiet rooms.

The external transmitter is attached to the internal receiver by a magnet.

Sounding old

As you enter old age, the cells in your inner ear that sense sound, known as hair cells, deteriorate and die off. This leads to partial or even complete deafness. Without these cells the link between your ear and brain is broken.

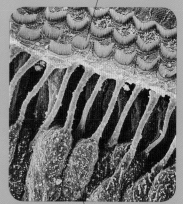

Fine "hairs" that detect sound

hair cell

Virtual reality

The holy grail of all sensory futures is the virtual reality machine. The early promises of a complete gaming experience with surround sound, sight, smell, and even touch, have long faded from computer companies' lips. But is virtual reality a forgotten dream? In an online world, consumers are bypassing long lines and shopping more online, so computer companies are leaving gaming behind and looking into "virtual touch" devices to help customers "feel" what they are buying. The emergency services and armed forces already use virtual reality simulators to train staff in extreme situations like terrorist attacks and natural disasters.

Virtual reality gaming has been in the pipeline for decades, but no devices have yet reached the stores.

Air traffic control towers could use virtual reality to help controllers visualize incoming airplane trajectories.

MICRO medicine

The medicine of the future

will involve less exploratory surgery and more therapies that target individual cells. Using nanomaterials and microtechnologies, many injuries and illnesses will be dealt with from inside the body.

Red blood cell

White blood cell

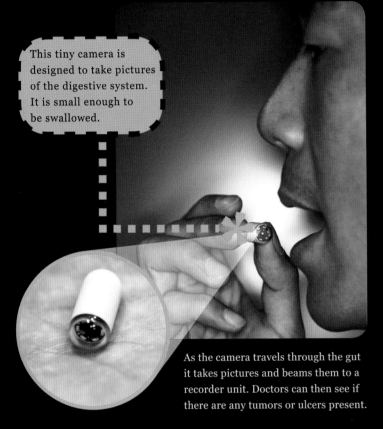

This tiny camera is designed to take pictures of the digestive system. It is small enough to be swallowed.

As the camera travels through the gut it takes pictures and beams them to a recorder unit. Doctors can then see if there are any tumors or ulcers present.

Nanoshells are tiny spheres coated with gold that can be engineered to respond to infrared light. Scientists have been using them to kill tumors. The nanoshells collect in the cancer cells. When an infrared light is switched on, the shells heat up and kill the cancer, leaving healthy cells undamaged.

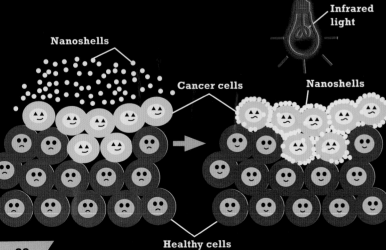

Nanoshells

Cancer cells

Infrared light

Nanoshells

Healthy cells

Nanorobots are tiny machines. One day they could be used inside the body to destroy blood clots or maintain blood vessels. Equipped with tiny lasers and instruments, they could repair cells and organs that humans are too clumsy to manage with their hands.

Under the skin

Micro- and nano-technologies are too small to be seen with the naked eye, but that makes them perfect for dealing with cells and molecules in the body.

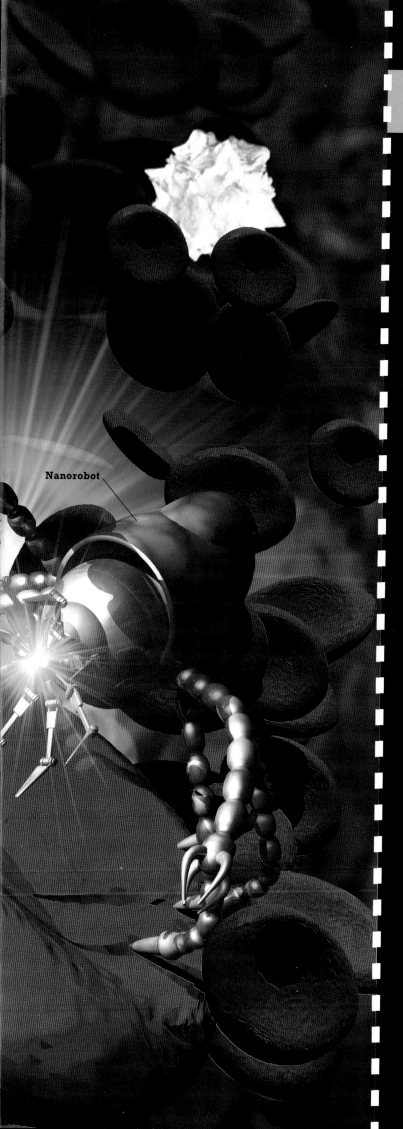

Nanorobot

This microchip is being tested with human cells to see if they react. Chips like this could be used to control implantable devices in parts of the body, such as the brain or eye, to restore function.

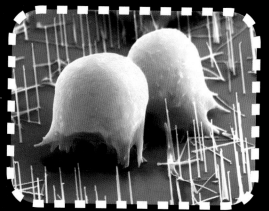

Stem cells are being grown on nanowires that relay electrical signals. The signals tell the stem cells how to develop, so that they grow into neurons, heart cells, or other specialized cells that are needed to repair damaged organs.

Silver nanoparticles are being used in wound dressings to help injuries to heal. Silver has an antibacterial effect, and tiny particles can penetrate the wound to stop it becoming badly infected.

Sun screens and other cosmetics often use nanoparticles that can penetrate the top layers of the skin. Some scientists are becoming concerned that they could also enter the bloodstream, which could lead to tissue damage.

So what does the future of body science hold? Maybe we are on track to embrace technology fully and will soon turn into robots. Sounds like science fiction? Books, movies, and TV are full of future visions of robots, androids, and replicants—so check them out!

Glossary

acceleration
A change in velocity. Acceleration happens when things speed up, slow down, or move in a different direction.

actin
One of the building blocks of muscle fibers that plays a key role in contraction.

adrenal glands
Glands located on top of the kidneys that make the hormone epinephrine (adrenaline).

aerobic
Describes a chemical process that requires oxygen to generate energy.

air pressure
The weight of the air pushing down on Earth. The more air pushing down, the higher the pressure.

algae
Tiny plantlike organisms that make food by the process of photosynthesis.

alveoli
Tiny sacs in the lungs through which oxygen and carbon dioxide pass to and from the bloodstream.

amino acids
The basic building blocks that make all proteins.

anaerobic
Describes a chemical process that does not require oxygen to make energy.

antagonist
Term describes the muscle that relaxes and stretches during movement of a joint.

antibodies
Cells of the immune system that are designed to locate and tag specific germs.

arteries
Blood vessels that carry oxygen-rich blood.

ATP (adenosine triphosphate)
The chemical molecule used by cells to make energy.

bacteria
Single-celled microorganisms that can be helpful or harmful to the body.

bionics
The application of technology to living systems—for example, artificial body parts.

bladder
The organ that collects and stores urine.

brain stem
The basic, core part of the brain that controls functions such as breathing and heart beat.

buoyancy
The upward force exerted on an object submerged in a liquid.

capillaries
Tiny blood vessels that branch off from arteries and veins.

carbon dioxide (CO2)
A waste gas produced when we breathe.

cell membranes
Thin fatty layers that surround cells.

cilia
Tiny hairlike cells in the nasal cavity and lungs.

cochlea
A snail-shaped, fluid-filled organ of the inner ear that helps process sound waves.

concentration (of solution)
The strength of a mixture of substances.

cramps
Painful muscle spasms.

density
The degree to which particles of matter are closely packed.

diffusion
The movement of a substance from an area of high concentration to one of low concentration.

DNA (deoxribo-nucleic acid)
The molecule that contains genes—the blueprints of life.

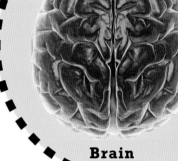

Brain

elasticity
The ability of a substance to return to its original shape after being stretched.

electrons
Negatively charged particles that revolve around the nucleus of an atom.

embryos
Organisms in the earliest stages of development.

epinephrine
A hormone released into the bloodstream in response to danger and stress.

estrogen
A female sex hormone.

evolution
The gradual development of living things over a long period of time.

force
A push or a pull that makes an object move or stop.

fossil fuels
Fuels formed over millions of years from the remains of animals and plants.

fuels
Substances that are used to produce energy.

gastric juices
Fluids the stomach produces to break down food.

genes
The instructions found in cells that make you you.

gravity
A force that pulls objects together. On Earth it keeps us stuck to the ground.

hormones
Chemicals that help control body functions such as growth and reproduction.

invertebrates
Animals without a backbone.

iris
The ring of colored muscle around the pupil in the eye.

laser
A form of intense light on one wavelength.

lens
The part of the eye that focuses light onto the retina.

lubrication
Reducing the friction between two surfaces.

mammals
Warm-blooded animals that feed their young with milk.

metabolism
All the chemical reactions that take place inside your body.

microchip
The part of a computer made from silicon on which tiny electronic circuits are etched.

molecules
Combinations of at least two atoms held together by chemical bonds.

momentum
The product of an object's mass and velocity.

MRI
Magnetic resonance imaging makes it possible for medical body scanners to produce pictures of your insides using powerful magnets and radio waves.

myosin
One of the building blocks of muscle fibers that makes them contract.

neurotransmitters
Chemicals that help nerve signals move across the tiny gaps between nerve cells.

nuclear reactions
Reactions involving the nuclei of atoms.

nucleus
The dense center of an atom or a cell.

nutrients
Substances your body needs to live and grow.

odorants
Molecules floating in the air that we detect as smells.

organs
Collections of cells and tissues that work together to do the same job.

osmosis
Movement of water through a membrane from an area of high concentration to an area of low concentration.

photosynthesis
The process by which plants use sunlight to convert carbon dioxide and water into carbohydrates and oxygen.

plasma (blood)
The colorless watery fluid in the blood that contains no cells.

plasma (state of matter)
The fourth state of matter in which a gas exists as charged particles.

prime mover
Term describing the muscle that contracts and shortens during movement.

prosthetics
The branch of medicine that deals with the manufacture of artificial body parts.

protons
Positively charged particles that are found in the nuclei of all atoms.

radioactivity
The process by which unstable atoms break apart, releasing energy in the process.

retina
The photosensitive lining at the back of the eye where light waves are focused.

sterilization
Protecting against infection by cleaning and disinfecting.

subatomic particles
The particles that make up an atom.

temperature
How hot or cold something is.

testosterone
A male sex hormone.

tissues
Collections of cells that work together to do the same job.

vertebrae
Small bones that make up the spine.

viruses
Tiny particles that invade cells and reproduce inside them.

viscosity
The thickness of a fluid.

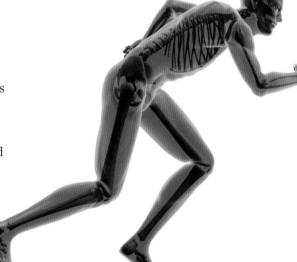

Index

Acknowledgments

The publisher would like to thank the following for their kind permission to reproduce their photographs:

(Key: a-above; b-below/bottom; c-center; f-far; l-left; r-right; t-top)

Alamy Images: Andy Day 66bl, 66fbl; Everynight Images / Lee Vincent Grubb 66fclb; Extreme Sports Photo 9b, 9t, 46-47, 66-67; Chris Howes / Wild Places Photography 36cl; James Nesterwitz 65t; Photo Researchers 62tl; Pictorial Press Ltd 35fbr; Trip 71bl; Martyn Vickery 83cr. **Corbis:** 48fcr; Theo Allofs / Zefa 23 (cracked ground); Heide Benser / Zefa 22 (water); David Bergman 60; Bettmann 52clb; Alessandro Bianchi / Reuters 84-85; Tom Brakefield 59crb (gazelle), 59fcrb (cheetah); Gareth Brown / Comet 54bc; China Daily / Reuters 6b, 32-33; Michael Cole 49br; Pascal Deloche / Godong 48cra; DK Limited / Christopher Cooper 19fbr; Duomo 53c; Randy Faris 62-63; Randy Faris / Flirt 19tr (teeth); Najlah Feanny / Corbis Saba 81fbl; Martin Harvey 64crb; image100 48cl; Dimitri Iundt / TempSport 70br; Jan-Peter Kasper / DPA 85cr; Kulka / Zefa 12-13; Matthias Kulka / Zefa 91fcra; Floris Leeuwenberg / The Cover Story 87br; Robert Llewellyn / Zefa 25ftr; Lyon and Amiens hospitals / Handou / Reuters 83cla; Lyon and Amiens hospitals / Handout / Reuters 83fcla; MedicalRF.com 27cr, 56fclb, 58fbr, 67r; Micro Discovery 24cb; Paul Miller / EPA 63bc; Tara Moore / Zefa 55cla; Jim Naughten 49c; David A. Northcott 59crb (lion); Louie Psihoyos 86cr; Louie Psihoyos / Comet 26fbl; Andy Rain / EPA 7b, 76-77; Jason Reed / Reuters 85br; Reuters 86bl; Lew Robertson / Flame 29cb (nails); Pascal Rossignol / Reuters 83ca; Southern Stock / Brand X 89bc; George Steinmetz 15fcra; Visuals Unlimited 54cra; William Whitehurst / Comet 90; Nation Wong / Zefa 16tr; Ira Wyman / Sygma 85tr; Bernd G. Schmitz / Zefa 68-69c. **DK Images:** Denoyer - Geppert Intl 27fcla (kidneys); ESPL / Denoyer-Geppert 27fcl (brain), 35clb, 38fcla; Jeremy Hunt - modelmaker 47 (shark); David Peart 69bc. **Fluent Inc.:** Fluent 63tr. **Getty Images:** 3D4Medical.com 40fcla, 43br, 45cr; 82fclb; Allsport Concepts / Mike Powell 55fcr; Blend Images / JGI 48fclb; Digital Vision 49cr; Digital Vision / Michael Hitoshi 48fcrb, 49cra, 49fcr; Digital Vision / Thomas Northcut 49fcla; DK Stock / Christina Kennedy 54cla; Gallo Images Roots Rf Collection / Clinton Friedman 48fcla; Iconica / Jeffrey Coolidge 49ca, 49cla; Iconica / PM Images 48crb, 49fbr; The Image Bank / Francesco Reginato 53t; Johner Images 54fcl; Jason Kempin / FilmMagic 83clb; Nucleus Medical Art, Inc. 21cl; NucleusMedicalArt.com / Nucleus Medical Art, Inc. 55fbr; OJO Images / Steve Smith 49bl; Photodisc / Thomas Northcut 75crb; Photographer's Choice - Bob Thomas 20-21; Photographer's Choice / Chemistry / Mark Langridge 49bc; Photographer's Choice / Oliver Cleve 35fcla, 40ftr; Photographer's Choice RR / Geri Lavrov 49cb; Photonica / Tommy Flynn 43c; Gary M Prior 8t; Riser / Andrew Geiger 70bl; Riser / Michael Melford 59br (elephant); Riser / Southern Stock 48clb; Science Faction / Tony Hallas 68t; Stockbyte 48c; Stockbyte / American Images Inc 49tr; Stockbyte / George Doyle 48cb, 49tc; StockFood Creative / Jeff Shaffer / Dawn Smith 49tl; Stone / Dominic DiSaia 59fcra; Stone / Dwight Eschliman 42fcl; Stone / Ed Freeman 55clb; Stone / Erik Dreyer 48bl; Stone / Gandee Vasan 75fcra; Stone / GK Hart / Vikki Hart 49ftr; Stone+ / Lars Borges 55cra; Stringer / AFP 70-71; Taxi / Johannes Kroemer 49fcrb; Taxi / Lester Lefkowitz 82c; Taxi / Richard Price 49fclb, 82fcr; Taxi / Shalom Ormsby 49fcl; Taxi / Steve Fitchett 8b, 40-41; Taxi / Tim McGuire 53b. **Gunther von Hagens' BODY WORLDS, Institute for Plastination, Heidelberg, Germany, www.bodyworlds.com:** 57. **iStockphoto.com:** Angelhell 92crb; Olivier Blondeau 44fbr; Leon Bonaventura 18; DSGpro 36tc; Murat Şen 19cr (pink measure); Marcus Lindström 37fcra; Kiyoshi Takahase Segundo 37clb; Jacom Stephens 19c (beaker). **The Natural History Museum, London:** 38-39. **Photolibrary:** 24r; Corbis 15tr; Photodisc / PhotoLink PhotoLink 69tl. **Science Photo Library:** 26cr (fat cells), 73tl, 80cla; David Becker 26cr (nerve cell); Biology Media 73fcr; Dr. Tony Brain 73ftr; BSIP 26cra (eye cell); BSIP Estiot 22cla; BSIP, Duval 87tc; BSIP, Vero / Carlo 41fcra; Andy Crump 88cl, 88fcl; Kevin Curtis 82crb; Colin Cuthbert 89cra; Martin Dohrn 40fcra; Michael Donne, University Of Manchester 79tc; Jim Dowdalls 23fclb; Equinox Graphics 86crb; Eye Of Science 44c, 63cr, 63fcr, 70c; Mauro Fermariello 81fcl; Peter Gardiner 67br; Prof. S.h.e. Kaufmann & Dr J.r Golecki 73fcl; Steve Gschmeissner 22fcr, 25cb, 26bc (skin cells), 54fcrb, 73cl; Gustoimages 7t, 50-51; Health Protection Agency 29crb (green bottle); Nancy Kedersha / UCLA 26crb (brain cells); Russell Kightley 73cr; James King-Holmes 87cra; Ton Kinsbergen 29crb (walnuts); Ted Kinsman 6t, 10-11; Chris Knapton 81ftr; Mehau Kulyk 27fclb (stomach); Dr. Najeeb Layyous 82ftr; Dr. P. Marazzi 89crb; Andrew McClenaghan 86fcl; Peter Menzel 87bc; NIBSC 73tr; Susumu Nishinaga 80fcr, 87fcra; Ria Novosti 28bl; Alfred Pasieka 23cla; Pasieka 25l, 27fcla (lungs); Alain Pol, ISM 23crb, 27fbl (bladder); Cheryl Power 21crb, 26ca (blood cells); Victor De Schwanberg 19tc (brain), 19tc (heart), 19tr (ear), 19tr (lips); Seymour 14tl; Jane Shemilt 87tl; Martin Shields 19tc (skull); Tek Image 79bc; Tim Vernon, LTH NHS Trust 87fcla; Victor Habbick Visions 88-89; Peidong Yang, Lawrence Berkeley National Laboratory 89c. **Shutterstock:** Andraž Cerar 29br.

Jacket images: Front: Getty Images: tr. **Back: Corbis:** Alessandro Bianchi / Reuters clb; Andy Rain / EPA cra. **Getty Images:** Iconica / Joel Kiesel cla. **Photolibrary:** Digital Vision / StockTrek StockTrek cr.

All other images © Dorling Kindersley
For further information see: www.dkimages.com

Respiratory system

Because your body needs a continual supply of oxygen, you breathe around 20,000 times a day. The respiratory system draws this oxygen into your bloodstream across the lungs' inner surfaces; carbon dioxide is released as a waste product. Your lungs and air passages make up the respiratory system.

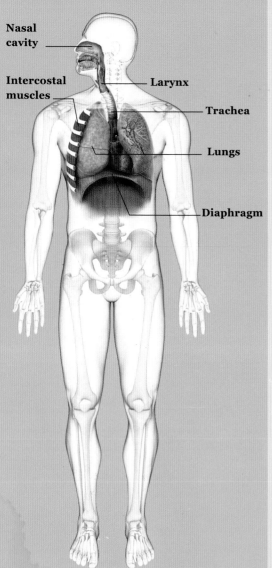

Nasal cavity

Intercostal muscles

Larynx

Trachea

Lungs

Diaphragm

Components checklist

- Nasal cavity
- Larynx
- Trachea
- Lungs
- Diaphragm

Cardiovasular system

To fight off infection and to stay alive, your cardiovascular system works hard to supply food and oxygen to your cells as well as removing waste matter. It does this by transporting substances, such as oxygen, in your blood along the network of tubes known as blood vessels. Arteries are shown in red, veins in blue.

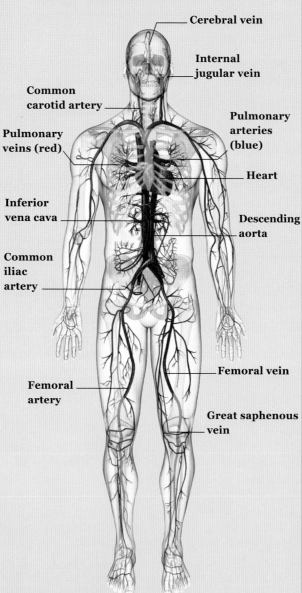

Cerebral vein

Internal jugular vein

Common carotid artery

Pulmonary arteries (blue)

Pulmonary veins (red)

Heart

Inferior vena cava

Descending aorta

Common iliac artery

Femoral vein

Femoral artery

Great saphenous vein

Components checklist

- Cerebral vein
- Common carotid artery
- Internal jugular vein
- Heart
- Pulmonary arteries and veins
- Inferior vena cava
- Descending aorta
- Common iliac artery
- Femoral artery and vein
- Great saphenous vein
- Blood

Nervous system

The nervous system configures your entire body's control structure. Consisting of the brain, spinal cord, and nerves, the nervous system carries high-speed electrical signals, called nerve impulses, around your body. These ensure you keep breathing and carry out hundreds of other essential tasks without even realizing it.

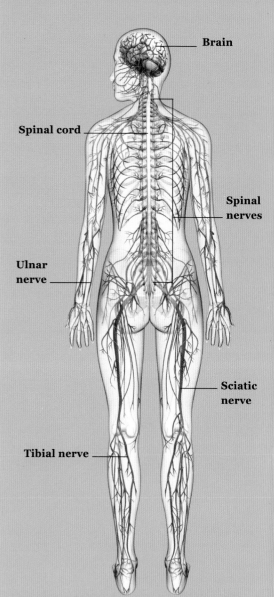

Brain

Spinal cord

Spinal nerves

Ulnar nerve

Sciatic nerve

Tibial nerve

Components checklist

- Brain
- Spinal cord
- Spinal nerves
- Ulnar nerve
- Sciatic nerve
- Tibial nerve